VALENCIA
POCKET GUIDE

Walking Eye
mobile app

Discover the world's best destinations with the Insight Guides Walking Eye app, available to download for free in the App Store and Google Play.

The container app provides easy access to fantastic free content on events and activities taking place in your current location or chosen destination, with the possibility of booking, as well as the regularly-updated Insight Guides travel blog: Inspire Me. In addition, you can purchase curated, premium destination guides through the app, which feature local highlights, hotel, bar, restaurant and shopping listings, an A to Z of practical information and more. Or purchase and download Insight Guides eBooks straight to your device.

TOP 10 ATTRACTIONS

MIGUELETE TOWER
Climb the distinctive belltower of the cathedral. See page 31.

BARRIO DEL CARMEN
The most fashionable part of the city, both night and day. See page 36.

LAS FALLAS
A spectacular festival where sculpture meets fire. See page 89.

TORRES DE SERRANOS
A reminder of the medieval city. See page 50.

MERCADO CENTRAL
A temple for good food. See page 40.

MUSEO DE BELLAS ARTES
View their first-rate art collection. See page 52.

LA LONJA
A silk merchants' market dating from the 15th century. See page 41.

LA ALBUFERA
One of Spain's most important bird habitats. See page 70.

CIUTAT DE LES ARTS I LES CIÈNCIES
Valencia's 21st-century architectural showcase, with lots to see and do. See page 57.

MUSEO NACIONAL DE CERÁMICA
A visual feast inside and out. See page 42.

A PERFECT DAY

9.00am

Breakfast
Start your day in the splendidly tiled Horchateria Santa Catalina (Plaza Santa Catalina, 6). Its speciality is *horchata*, a sweet, milky drink made with tiger nuts usually drunk later in the day. A better choice for breakfast is a *café con leche* with an *ensaimada* (a soft, sweet bun).

11.00am

Towering view
Then make your way through the atmospheric old streets of the Barrio del Carmen to the cathedral and climb its belfry, the Miguelete, for an unbeatable panoramic view over the city's rooftops.

10.00am

Medieval streets and Gothic architecture
For a tour of the old part of the city, head first for the Mercado Central, a glorious art nouveau market hall where you'll see Valencia at its liveliest, and then cross the road to the graceful Gothic hall of La Lonja.

12 noon

To the seaside
Walk up the road from the Plaza de la Virgen, behind the cathedral, to the river bank near the Torres del Serrano. Cross the pedestrian bridge in front of you to get to the tram station. Take line 4 to the port and have a stroll around the quayside, redeveloped for the America's Cup.

IN VALENCIA

4.00pm

Futuristic architecture
Catch metro line 5 to Alameda and walk up the river bank to the extraordinary gleaming white buildings of the Ciutat de les Arts i les Ciències. Looking like something out of a sci-fi movie, the City of Arts and Sciences is modern architecture at its most striking.

10.00pm

A night out
Have dinner in stylish Ricard Camarena Restaurant (Avda. Burjassot 54) and follow it with a nightcap in one of the many bars in the Barrio del Carmen. This is a good place to sample the city's nightlife, but don't get there too early as the action doesn't get going properly until after midnight.

2.00pm

Paella lunch
Enjoy Valencia's signature dish with a long lazy paella lunch (ordered in advance) at La Pepica, or any other restaurant on the Paseo Neptuno which backs on to the beach.

7.00pm

Time for tapas
Head back to the centre and join the throngs converging on the city's tapas bars for an evening drink and snack. One of the best is Bar Pilar (Moro Zeit, 13) which has been going since 1912 and is renowned for its mussels.

CONTENTS

- **INTRODUCTION** 10
- **A BRIEF HISTORY** 14
- **WHERE TO GO** 25

City centre 25
Plaza del Ayuntamiento 26, Plaza de la Reina and Plaza Redonda 28, The cathedral 29, Plaza de la Virgen 34, Barrio del Carmen 36, The market and La Lonja 39, Museo de Cerámica 42, The university and El Patriarca 45

Along the River Turia 47
The upper Turia 48, Museo de Bellas Artes 52, Los Viveros and beyond 52, The final stretch 55

The City of Arts and Sciences 56
Palau de les Arts 57, L'Hemisfèric 58, Museu de les Ciències Príncipe Felipe 58, L'Umbracle 59, L'Oceanogràfic 59

The seafront 60
The port 62, The Paseo de Neptuno and Paseo Marítimo 63, The Cabanyal 65,

Around the city 66
The huerta 66, La Albufera 69, Ceramics towns 71, El Puig Monastery 72

Excursions 73
Sagunt 73, Peñíscola 74, Gandía 75, Xàtiva (Játiva) 77, Denia and Jávea (Xàbia) 78

WHAT TO DO 81

Shopping 81
Entertainment 86
Fiestas 88
Sports 92
Valencia for children 94

EATING OUT 96

A–Z TRAVEL TIPS 113

RECOMMENDED HOTELS 137

DICTIONARY 143

INDEX 166

FEATURES

Hosting the America's Cup 12
Legacy of the Moors 16
Historical landmarks 23
The city's symbol 27
Via Augusta 28
Valencia's Holy Grail 32
Visiting the City of Arts and Sciences 56
Birds of La Albufera 71
The upside-down king 77
The language of the fan 85
The Fallas makers 91
Calendar of events 95
Paella etiquette 98

INTRODUCTION

If Valencians have a reputation in Spain for being a fortunate, rather blasé people, perhaps it isn't so surprising. Spain's third-largest city after Madrid and Barcelona, Valencia has a more privileged natural setting, a more agreeable climate and, consequently, arguably a better standard of living than either.

Founded by the Romans 2,000 years ago, it stands on a shallow scoop of a bay half-way down the Mediterranean coast. Curiously, however, the city wasn't founded on the coast but a little way inland. Valencia, it always used to be said, had its back to the sea; with its commercial and fishing port kept at an avenue's length from the city centre, so that it is possible to wander around without any sense of being by the seaside.

Neither does the city stand on a river – at least, not any more. It may have grown up on the right bank of the Turia, which flows off the high plateau in the centre of Spain into the Mediterranean, but after a disastrous flood in 1957, the decision was taken to divert the river along an artificial channel around the outer suburbs. You can still walk along the banks of what was the Turia, but you won't be walking beside a river. Ingeniously, the redundant course has been turned into an attractive feature of a different kind: an

Dual roles

Valencia is a city of over 790,000 people. It is both the capital of a province of the same name and of an autonomous region, the Comunidad Valenciana, which stretches from the borders of Catalonia to the southern reaches of the Costa Blanca. Both city and region are bilingual with Valencian – a softer form of Catalan – enjoying equal status with Spanish (Castilian).

elongated ribbon of parks and sports fields crossed by a mix of historic and strikingly new bridges.

It might not be on the sea and no longer on a river, but Valencia still remains the hub of a prodigiously fertile plain, the *huerta*, an intricate mesh of market gardens, orange groves and rice fields. The harvest wealth from these fields has always been the foundation for Valencia's prosperity and self-confidence, and the debt is duly acknowledged. Everywhere you look in the city there are motifs of fruits, flowers and a balmy country life glorified in stone and stained glass, but above all in the brilliance of multicoloured ceramic tiles.

All smiles at the Mercado Central

VALENCIA TRANSFORMED

Yet for all its natural advantages, Valencia has never been well known abroad and until recently has received less than its fair share of foreign visitors. This is not for want of attractive qualities. Monuments it has aplenty – especially glorious Gothic buildings dating from its 15th-century heyday when it was one of the most prosperous mercantile cities in Europe. Museums and art galleries it has too, as well as gardens, elegant public squares and grand avenues lined with palms and massive ficus trees. All this in a compact, easily walkable city centre that was largely bypassed by tourists through ignorance rather than intent.

Not any more. The city is in the grip of a new spirit for self-improvement and self-promotion. While the run-down Barrio del Carmen quarter has been transformed into a trendy place to spend a leisurely day's sightseeing or a night crawling between bars, one of the boldest architectural initiatives in Europe, the City of Arts and Sciences, has taken shape in the reclaimed bed of the river.

Everywhere you look, Valencia is busy re-fashioning itself – laying out new avenues and metro lines, remodelling the old and building new hotels, bridges and shopping complexes. Its port was given a facelift to receive the America's Cup.

LIVING THE GOOD LIFE

What is really striking about contemporary Valencia is not that it is bristling with new buildings, offices and infrastructure, but that it is learning to show off and share the simple, good things its people have always enjoyed. Living the good life is turning out to be the city's most marketable commodity.

Proof of this begins in the huge central market, which receives the unstoppable quantities of fresh produce that pour into the city daily. Valencian cuisine makes straightforward use of this

⊙ HOSTING THE AMERICA'S CUP

Thanks to its excellent wind and wave conditions, its existing facilities and its potential for development, Valencia was selected to host the 32nd America's Cup in 2007, a decision which greatly enhanced the city's esteem and led to a frenzy of building: the port was split in two with one side dedicated to commerce and the other to leisure. The prestige and facilities that came with the America's Cup have put Valencia on the Spanish tourist map in the same league as Madrid, Barcelona and Seville.

abundance in a range of rice dishes, outstanding among them being Spain's national dish, paella. Invented in the *huerta*, a well-prepared paella is both colourful and appetising: it looks as good as it tastes. In restaurants all over Valencia you can eat the real thing – perhaps even cooked in the traditional way over a wood fire.

Then there is the nightlife, the so-called Moon of Valencia. In such a benign climate it's easy to go out late and stay out late, with or without kids in tow. The extrovert parade around well-known zones of proliferating *pubs*, while anyone in search of a less raunchy time can cherry-pick from among a decent range of more sedate and sophisticated bars and cafés.

Valencia also boasts some of Spain's most showy fiestas. The Fallas in March, a riotous week of non-stop noise and commotion culminates with the burning of giant comic sculptures in narrow streets and teeming squares.

If you tire of the urban pace, there are sandy beaches to relax on; quieter towns in the Valencian hinterland to explore; and luxuriant countryside to breathe in at the edge of the city.

It's no cliché to say that Valencia is a place where the senses are constantly being stimulated: there is rarely a moment of silence nor something worth looking at. If Valencians have a tendency towards sensuality and hedonism who can blame them, and who wouldn't want to join them for at least a while?

Plaza del Ayuntamiento

A BRIEF HISTORY

Although, as innumerable archaeological finds attest, the uplands of eastern Spain have been continuously inhabited since the Stone Age, the city of Valencia itself is of comparatively recent origin. It was founded, as Valentia, in 138BC by the Roman consul Decimus Junius Brutus to accommodate legionnaires who had served in the victorious campaign against the Lusitanians in the west of the Iberian peninsula. He chose as a site an island in the River Turia roughly equidistant between the two important Roman cities of Tarraco (Tarragona) and Cartago Nova (Cartagena). The place was marshy and inhospitable but easily defended against attacks by local tribes of Celtiberians.

As Valentia grew and thrived, its early tents and huts were replaced by mud and stone houses protected by a wall. But all this was destroyed by Pompey in 75BC as he waged civil war against Sertorius. The settlement was abandoned for almost 50 years before being reoccupied. This time it grew more securely, acquiring a forum, baths, circus, river port and systematic water supply. When the Roman Empire began to decline, however, Valentia declined with it. Its public buildings fell into disuse and entire suburbs were depopulated.

In the 4th century, a Christian community was established around the memory of St Vincent who was tortured and martyred here in 304.

Gradually, as the Church grew in power and

El Cid

According to legend, when El Cid died in 1099, the Moors were besieging Val-encia but the sight of his body being led out of the city propped up on a horse was enough to make the attackers panic. They fled the city.

importance, the ecclesiastical authorities assumed the governance of the city. However, in the mid-6th century Valencia came under the sway of the Visigoths, former allies of Rome.

MUSLIM VALENCIA

In 711 Muslim invaders from North Africa – the Moors – defeated the Visigoths and in the following years overran Spain. There is little documentary evidence from Valencia

El Cid, Spain's national hero

(Balansiya at that time), but it is known that the emir of Cordoba, Abd al-Rahman, sacked the city in 778 to put down a rebellion and that his son Abd allah al-Balansi built a palace in what is now the suburb of Russafa. Islam became the dominant religion – although Christianity and Judaism were tolerated – and Arabic the language of official transactions and daily life. When the caliphate of Cordoba disintegrated in 1010, Balansiya became the capital of an independent kingdom or *taifa*.

At the end of the 11th century the Christian warrior Rodrigo Díaz de Vivar, better known as El Cid, captured Balansiya and briefly ruled it as his own fief. Shortly after his death it was recaptured by an Arab army and was to remain a Muslim city for over 130 years.

Islam was not, however, to retain its foothold in Europe forever, and the Christian reconquerors of Spain made steady progress south. As they approached Balansiya, the city's defences were strengthened, but on 9 October 1238 the city fell to Jaime (James) I, king of Catalonia and Aragón, bringing it into the mainstream of European civilisation. Under Jaime I, Muslim possessions were shared among Christian barons and the city became the capital of a new kingdom of Valencia, under the aegis of the crown of Aragón. Valencia was granted its own *furs*: laws guaranteeing its right to self-governance with its own institutions and currency.

THE MIDDLE AGES

Although the 14th century was a traumatic time for Valencia, being punctuated by rebellion, war and the Black Death, it was also a time of growth as immigrants arrived in large numbers to work in the textile industry. By the end of the century, Valencia was entering its golden age, a period of prosperity built on enterprise and trade. As one of the most important ports on the Mediterranean – indeed one of the most important cities in Europe – it became the most populous city in Spain, a cosmopolitan, mercantile and financial metropolis. Its docks

⊘ LEGACY OF THE MOORS

Although the Moors ruled Valencia effectively for over four centuries, few monuments have survived from that time; but they did leave something of much more lasting significance, the *huerta*. This intensely cultivated alluvial plain, which takes over where the suburbs end, is still irrigated by an ingenious system of dams and channels created by Moorish farmers to feed the prodigiously productive orchards and market gardens. Here they cultivated the crops they had brought with them to Spain: rice, sugar cane, cotton, saffron, oranges, lemons and mulberry trees (the food plant of silkworms).

Map of the Valencian region, 1640

would be busy unloading Genoese and Venetian ships which had arrived laden with Italian fabrics, gold and slaves from Africa and which would depart replete with wool, leather, ceramics and the produce of the *huerta*. The most emblematic building surviving from this time is the silk exchange of La Lonja, looking more like a temple than a trading floor.

The flow of wealth provided for a simultaneous flowering in the arts and learning: some of the first print shops in Spain were set up and the university was founded. This was also the time of two influential Valencian writers: the poet Ausias March and Joanot Martorell, the knight-author of *Tirant lo Blanc*, a novel of chivalry praised by Cervantes as 'the best book of its kind in the world'.

Despite economic and cultural prosperity, however, social, economic, religious and political tensions were building and these exploded into revolt in 1519 when the *germanías* – brotherhoods of artisans, peasants, the petty bourgeoisie and low-ranking clergy – rose up against the nobility and took control of the city. Civil war spread across the kingdom and the revolt was put down by a repressive Spanish monarchy anxious to assert its centralising authority on the regions of a newly unified Spain.

EXPULSION OF THE MOORS

There was, however, a further crisis building as the Counter-Reformation took hold in Spain. Although many Muslims had fled Valencia when it had been reconquered, many others had stayed and continued their way of life under Christian rule, accepting nominal conversion to Christianity. The Moriscos, as they were known, made up a sizeable proportion of Valencia's population. Many continued to observe the tenets of Islam in secret, wore Muslim costume and spoke Arabic. Royal decrees issued in 1525–6 sought to prohibit these lingering vestiges of Muslim Spain but, as the nobles of Valencia were economically dependent on the craft skills and labour of the Moriscos, they protected them from the Inquisition and for decades the decrees were not effectively enforced. When, at last, the Moors were expelled from Spain by Felipe (Philip) III in 1609, Valencia is estimated to have lost almost a third of its workforce, leaving some villages without inhabitants and depriving key industries – notably that of silk-making – of their most skilled workers.

Just over a century later, Valencia again became disastrously embroiled in national politics. The death of King Carlos III without an heir divided the country – and Europe – between supporters of the Bourbon pretender Felipe V and Archduke Charles of Austria, who arrived in Spain in 1707 to claim the crown. Valencia sided with the latter but when Charles's supporters were defeated at the Battle of Almansa on 25 April 1707, the victorious Felipe took revenge with a decree abolishing the autonomous status of

Valencia as enshrined centuries before in the *furs*. A garrison of soldiers was installed in the city and a mostly Castilian aristocracy took over its administration.

INDUSTRIALISATION

The 19th century was also a turbulent time for Spain, beginning with invasion. In the aftermath of the French Revolution the country was plunged into the Peninsular War (known in Spain as the War of Independence), and Valencia was twice besieged and occupied for a year and a half by the troops of Napoleon under General Suchet. Following the departure of French forces, the liberals of Spain enjoyed a brief ascendancy before Fernando (Ferdinand) VII disembarked at Valencia, declaring the restoration of the absolutist Bourbon monarchy and ushering in a period of repression. Fernando's death sparked a crisis of succession and for seven years the country was ruled by the regent María Cristina until she was forced out of power, departing from Valencia into exile in 1840. The struggle between liberalism and conservatism, royalists and republicans, went on for the rest of the century.

18th-century tiles

Notwithstanding events in Madrid, the Valencian economy grew and matured during the 19th century. The city rapidly industrialised. As steam engines gradually began to power factories, increasing output, so wage-labour replaced traditional artisan activities. Silk production, introduced 1,000 years before by the

> ### La Renaixença
>
> Spearheaded by writer Constanti Llomber and journalist Teodoro Llorente, the *Renaixença* (Renaissance) cultural movement arose in the 1870s to promote the literary worth of the Valencian language and the values of Valencian identity.

Moors, declined to make way for modern industries such as metallurgy, ceramics, chemicals and furniture-making – sucking in vast numbers of immigrants from the countryside. Between 1800 and 1900 the city's population grew from 50,000 to 215,000 and in the pressure to build houses, roads and railways it was decided, in 1865, to demolish the 4.5km (3 miles) of medieval city walls, creating work for potentially rebellious redundant silk factory workers. This was also a time of renaissance for Valencian regional identity, and the Valencian language and traditions regained respectability lost in centuries of centralisation.

THE CIVIL WAR

For all its economic growth, Spain began the 20th century with its political problems still unresolved. The installation of the Second Republic in 1931 brought hopes of greater democracy, land reform, and the recognition of regional identities in Spain, but opinion was fast polarising between revolution and reaction. Things came to a head on 17 July 1936 when military plotters led by General Francisco Franco launched a revolt against the elected government, thereby plunging the country into civil war. Franco's Nationalist uprising failed in large parts of the country, including Valencia, which sided with the beleaguered Republic.

For a time it seemed that either side might prevail. Early on, the Nationalist forces threatened to take Madrid, and in November 1936 the government moved to Valencia, which became the de-facto capital of Spain. The parliament was housed in the city hall and La Lonja, and the government in Benicarló Palace. As the Nationalists advanced after the fall of Catalonia, refugees poured into the city, which held out until the very end. Bombed, shelled from the sea and besieged, its fate seemed inevitable. On 30 March 1939, the day before the end of hostilities, Valencia was entered by Nationalist forces under General Aranda.

THE POST-WAR PERIOD

In the early years of Franco's regime, the whole of Spain suffered from shortages, hunger and economic paralysis, but Valencia, which had sided against the dictator, was also subjected to a centralising, homogenising force even more severe than that of the absolutist monarchs of old. It was deprived of political autonomy, and use of the Valencian language was prohibited. As if things weren't bad enough, in 1957 the River Turia broke its banks and caused serious flooding. The river was subsequently directed into a new, artificial course around the outside of the urban area.

Gradually, as Spain recovered economically during the 1960s, Valencia's standard of living rose and new blocks of flats were erected and motorways built, eating up the shrinking farmland of the *huerta*.

Tourist poster, 1930

Anti-Fascist demonstration in the city, 1937

MODERN VALENCIA

Franco's death in 1975 made way for a transition to democracy. On 23 February 1981 new-won freedoms were threatened by a coup d'etat launched by officers of the Guardia Civil. Ultimately the coup failed, but not before General Milans del Bosch ordered his tanks down the Gran Via of Valencia to point their guns at the headquarters of the Socialist Party.

The return of democracy brought with it the restoration of a large measure of autonomy to Spain's regions. The use of the Valencian language was now not only permitted but encouraged: it is taught in schools and given equal status to Spanish (Castilian) in all official documents.

Devolution also brought a recovery of regional pride, and since the mid 1980s the city has been getting a face lift. The once-seedy quarter of El Carmen has been gentrified. The bed of the River Turia has been turned into a ribbon of gardens and sports facilities. A modern metro and tramway have been laid out and the long-neglected beachfront has been treated to a broad new *paseo* (promenade) lined with palm trees. But the many new buildings have been eclipsed by the opening of the City of Arts and Sciences, an ambitious project worthy of any cultured European city. The neighbourhood of El Cabanyal is also being given a thorough revamp after years of neglect, while a new 'cycling ring' around the historic centre was inaugurated in 2017.

HISTORICAL LANDMARKS

138BC Valentia founded as colony for Roman legionnaires.
75BC Valentia destroyed by Pompey in his civil war against Sertorius.
AD304 St Vincent the Deacon is martyred in Valentia.
711 Moorish conquest of Spain.
778 Abd al-Rahman, emir of Cordoba, attacks and sacks the city.
1010 Balansiya becomes capital of a kingdom or *taifa*.
1094 El Cid takes Balansiya. In 1102 it falls again into Muslim hands.
1238 The city is conquered by Jaime I of Aragón-Catalonia.
1262 Foundation stone of Valencia cathedral laid.
1348 Black Death.
1474 Valencia becomes part of the Spanish state by the marriage of Fernando II of Aragón and Isabel of Castile.
1499 La Lonja completed; university founded.
1609 Expulsion of Moors from Spain by Felipe III.
1702–14 War of the Spanish Succession.
1707 Felipe V wins Battle of Almansa. Valencia loses its *furs* (privileges).
1812–13 Napoleonic occupation under Suchet.
1936–9 Spanish Civil War. The government abandons Madrid for Valencia in 1936. The city surrenders the day before the war ends.
1957 River Turia causes serious flooding.
1982 Valencia is granted autonomous statute.
2004 City of Arts and Sciences completed.
2007 America's Cup held in Valencia.
2011 Francisco Camps steps down as the Valentian premier (head of regional government) following allegations of involvement in the notorious Gürtel corruption case.
2015 Left-wing politician Joan Ribó becomes Valencia's mayor, succeeding the late Rita Barberá who held the post for 24 years and was subsequently accused of money laundering.
2017 The Spanish government, based in Madrid, clamps down on Catalonia's bid for independence.

Santiago Calatrava's stunning Palau de les Arts

WHERE TO GO

The city centre, bordered to the north by the dry bed of the River Turia, to the south by the railway station and to the east and west by broad avenues, is compact enough to walk around. Most of the major sights are contained within this area. The fine arts museum and Los Viveros gardens, however, are on the far bank of the Turia but still within easy reach of the centre on foot. To travel further afield there is an efficient bus network and a metro system which connects with a modern tramway to the beach. Another option is to hire a bike (see page 115) and take advantage of the city's flat terrain and network of cycle lanes.

CITY CENTRE

Whether or not you arrive by train, a good place to begin a tour of Valencia is the mainline railway station, the **Estación del Norte**. Built between 1907 and 1917 in a style inspired by Austrian art nouveau, it is far more than a mere transit terminal; this is a celebration of the agricultural abundance of Valencia. Its twin white towers are hung with bunches of sculpted oranges. Inside there are yet more oranges, this time in stained glass. In the foyer and cafeteria, meanwhile, are ceramic murals depicting the life and crops of the *huerta*, the farmland around Valencia.

Street names

Many streets and squares in Valencia have two versions of their name, in the Valencian language and in Spanish (Castilian). Also, some squares have changed their names within living memory and locals often still refer to them by their former names.

The town hall in the Plaza del Ayuntamiento

Over the road from the station is the 19th-century **Plaza de Toros**, four floors of 384 identical brick arches making a structure reminiscent of a Roman amphitheatre and with seats for 17,000 people. The bullfights here during the Fallas festival in March constitute the first of the official season. Next to it, in Pasaje Doctor Serra, is one of the oldest bullfighting museums in Spain, the **Museo Taurino** (www.museotaurinovalencia.es; Tue–Sat 10am–7pm, Sun and holidays 10am–2pm).

PLAZA DEL AYUNTAMIENTO

From the station it is only a short walk to the triangular main square, the **Plaza del Ayuntamiento**. Laid out in the 1920s, it has had four names during its short history. During Franco's time it was known in his honour as the Plaza del Caudillo but after his death, the citizens of Valencia were quick to remove the name and the statue of their defunct leader mounted proudly on a horse.

PLAZA DEL AYUNTAMIENTO

The main building presiding over the square is the **Ayuntamiento** ❶, the city hall (Mon–Fri 8am–3pm except on days of official functions; www.valencia.es; free), an ornate palace of municipal authority which is essentially two buildings in one. First came a convent-like girls' school, founded in the 19th century by the archbishop of Valencia. To this was added a dignified civic palace distinguished by its twin domes on the corner, a clock tower and a large ceremonial balcony placed in the middle. At the tower's base stand a statue of the city's coat of arms, and four statues representing Prudence, Fortitude, Justice and Temperance. Inside the city hall there is a handsome marble staircase, ornate council chamber and reception room, and municipal museum (open on weekdays 8am–2pm).

Across the square is the **post office** with sculpted angels, representing the speed of modern communications, hovering over its façade. The letter boxes at ground level are in the form of snarling bronze lions' heads.

If the centre of the square between these two buildings seems a little devoid of interest except for its flower stalls, it

⊙ THE CITY'S SYMBOL

In front of the city hall, at the base of the clock tower, is a statue of the city's coat of arms held by two naked females and surmounted by a bat. The bat (*rat penat* in Valencian, meaning 'winged rat') has been Valencia's symbol since the 13th century. In 1238, while Jaime I of Aragón was going about the business of conquering Moorish-held Valencia, a bat is supposed to have perched on his helmet. This was seen as an omen of good fortune and, ever since then, the bat has been retained as a symbol of the city.

CITY CENTRE

is because it is kept as a public space for fiestas. In particular, during the Fallas festival (see page 89), when the largest of the city's combustible works of art is erected here. Before and during the Fallas, the square is also used as the setting for a *mascletà*, a peculiarly Valencian tradition of letting off firecrackers in synch in broad daylight with the aim not of making pretty visual effects but of creating a deafening but – or so Valencians think – harmonious din.

PLAZA DE LA REINA AND PLAZA REDONDA

Continue out of the square via its apex, walking in the same direction in which you arrived, and you will join Calle San Vicente Mártir. This leads you towards the second most important square, the Plaza de la Reina. On your right you pass the Pasaje Ripalda, a shopping gallery with a glass roof. Take the alley on your left before you reach Plaza de la Reina and you will step into the charming **Plaza Redonda** ❷ ('Round Square'). This caprice of mid-19th-century urban development, inaccessible to cars, is known affectionately by the locals as el Clot (the Hole). Arranged around the fountain in the middle is a small

⊘ VIA AUGUSTA

Once Spain had been brought fully under Roman control, the Emperor Augustus (27BC–AD14) ordered a road to be built down the east coast, linking the Pyrenees and Cádiz. Named the Via Augusta after the emperor, it extended 1,500km (930 miles) and was the longest Roman road in the Iberian Peninsula. Although it was primarily intended to enable troop movements, it also facilitated trade. Its route runs through Sagunt to Valencia where it passes through the Plaza de la Reina in the centre of the city.

Plaza Redonda

ring of stalls specialising in haberdashery, ceramics and work clothes.

You can easily get lost exploring the maze of streets beyond the Plaza Redonda, but for now it is best to retrace your steps up the alley and continue into the **Plaza de la Reina** (formerly known as Plaza Zaragoza). As a taster before visiting the cathedral, which lies ahead of you, it is worth visiting the **Iglesia de Santa Catalina** ❸, impossible to miss because of its distinctive baroque belltower built on a hexagonal plan. The church proper inside is not baroque at all, but a pure and soothing Gothic. Near the entrance to the church, is one of Valencia's oldest *horchaterías* (see page 103): **Santa Catalina** (www.horchateriasantacatalina.com), with tiled decorations and marble tables.

THE CATHEDRAL

The top side of the Plaza de la Virgen is formed by Valencia's magnificent **Catedral** ❹ (winter: Mon–Sat 10am–5.30pm, Sun 2–5.30pm; summer Mon–Sat 10am–6.30pm, Sun 2–6.30pm; charge; www.catedraldevalencia.es), with its octagonal belltower, El Miguelete, rising above it. The foundation stone for the building was laid in 1262 on the site of a mosque, and although it was begun in the prevailing Romanesque style the majority of it is Gothic. You wouldn't think so, however, as you approach it up the square because the doorway before you, the **Puerta de Hierros**, is unrestrained baroque, the work of Konrad Rudolf, a German pupil of Bernini. Although this is the main façade, it looks cramped and uncomfortable because it had to be superimposed on a pre-existing building, with the immovable El Miguelete taking up much of the space.

To appreciate the simplicity of the cathedral it is best to skirt round it to the right and enter by the earliest doorway, the rounded Romanesque **Puerta del Palau**, which gives on to the Plaza del Palacio del Arzobispal. This has a pleasingly understated decoration. The 14 small heads under the cornice are said to represent seven men and their wives who came from Lerida to repopulate Valencia after the Christians had reconquered it from the Moors.

Once inside the cathedral you can fully appreciate its basic Gothic structure. The nave is now of clean stone – most of the extraneous 18th-century decoration having been removed in the 1980s.

It is lit by an elegant *cimborrio*, an ocatagonal, two-storey lantern which is pierced by windows of delicate tracery, the sunlight filtered through panes of alabaster.

The altar, however, is an elaborate accumulation of Renaissance and baroque art, the altarpiece being by two artists heavily influenced by Leonardo da Vinci. One grisly point of interest behind the altar is the brown and shrivelled mummified forearm of St Vincent the Deacon, co-patron of the city, who was martyred in Valencia in 304.

Altogether more beguiling is the cathedral's most famous relic, what is claimed to be the **Holy Grail**, the cup that Jesus Christ drank out of at the Last Supper. The small, dark red agate cup, which in the 14th century was set in a gold

The cathedral's Gothic nave

framework studded with jewels, is on display in a gloomy chapel, formerly a chapterhouse, beneath a roof of stellar vaulting sprouting from coloured bosses.

The Chapel of the Holy Grail gives access to the **cathedral museum** (https://museocatedralvalencia.com) which houses a few treasures, including some of the original polychrome statues, two paintings by Goya, other paintings by Juan de Juanes and a giant monstrance which is taken through the streets of Valencia during the procession of Corpus Christi.

The last thing to do before leaving the cathedral is to climb the octagonal belltower of the **Miguelete** (Micalet in Valencian; summer daily 10am–7.30pm, winter Mon–Sat 10am–6.30pm, Sun 10am–1pm and 5.30–7pm; extra charge), which demands the giddying ascent of a spiral staircase of more than 200 steps to a terrace over 50m (160ft) above the city streets below. The tower owes its name to having been consecrated on 29

CITY CENTRE

September 1418, the feast day of the archangel St Michael, Miguelete being the affectionately diminutive form of his name.

From the tower, peels rang across the city in the late Middle Ages announcing the times to open and close the city gates. The bellcote crowning the tower today is, however, a later addition.

Outside the cathedral

Leave the cathedral by the door opposite the main entrance, the **Puerta de los Apóstoles**, a triumph of 14th-century Gothic

> #### VALENCIA'S HOLY GRAIL
>
> Like Turin's shroud, the purported Holy Grail in Valencia's cathedral has been the subject of a great deal of speculation. In 1960, a professor of archaeology at Zaragoza University dismantled and examined the cup and proclaimed it to be of a date prior to Jesus Christ and made in a workshop of the Near East; but there is no evidence connecting it directly to New Testament events.
>
> According to legend it was taken from Jerusalem to Rome by Saint Peter and there used by popes to celebrate mass. When the Emperor Valerian persecuted the Church and tried to confiscate its treasures, San Lorenzo – the first deacon of the Church – dispatched the grail to Huesca, in the Pyrenean foothills, for safety, three days before being martyred for his faith. It now made its appearance in historical documents. During the Muslim conquest of the Iberian Peninsula, the grail was kept in the remote monastery of San Juan de la Peña.
>
> In 1437 it arrived in Valencia where it has been ever since, except during the Napoleonic occupation of Spain when it was smuggled out for safe-keeping.

sculpture attributed to Nicolás de Ancona. Looking behind you, you can admire the veritable crowd of Biblical characters gathered around the door, including 14 angels, 16 saints, 18 prophets and, to the sides of the door, the apostles standing on triangular pillars and sheltered by tabernacles. All these statues were originally coloured and kept repainted until at least 1522 when they began to be badly worn by the elements. The worst eroded were withdrawn in modern times and have been replaced with copies.

The Miguelete

Every Thursday at 12 noon this doorway becomes the setting for what is perhaps the most extraordinary court of law anywhere in the world. It is here that the **Water Court** (Tribunal de las Aguas) meets in public and in the open air to decide disputes between farmers over the use of irrigation water in the *huerta* around the city. The eight judges dressed in black smocks – all farmers themselves, elected by their peers – represent the different networks of water channels. Hearings are instant and oral (in Valencian): no records are taken; no appeal is possible: and no business is put off until another session. The court has met in this way weekly, with scarcely a break since 1239. When there is no debate the affair can be over while the clock is still striking midday – so get there promptly if you want to see it.

The fountain on Plaza de la Virgen

PLAZA DE LA VIRGEN

The Puerta de los Apóstoles lets you out into the **Plaza de la Virgen** (built on top of the Roman forum), which is now a car-free place to mill around, feed pigeons, or sit in a pavement café and watch life go by. In the middle of the square is a fountain representing the god Triton, personifying the River Turia, surrounded by eight figures with pitchers pouring water, representing the principal irrigation channels feeding the *huerta*.

The cathedral shares this square with two other impressive buildings. Beside the Puerta de los Apóstoles is what looks almost like a lost section of the Colosseum. This is an arcaded gallery belonging to the cathedral known as **Els Balconets de la Seu**, which serves as a dais from which church dignitaries can watch processions and other events taking place in the square. The most spectacular of these events is La Ofrenda, part of the Fallas festival in March, when a huge copy of the statue of Valencia's

PLAZA DE LA VIRGEN

patroness, the Virgen de los Desamparados (the Virgin of the Forsaken or Helpless), is made out of bunches of flowers brought by a lengthy procession of people dressed in traditional costume.

The actual statue of the Virgin is of a more modest size and form, although obscured by the wig, rich clothes and jewels that lavishly adorn her.

The statue is kept on display above the altar in the church dedicated to her, the 17th-century **Basílica de la Virgen de los Desamparados** (daily 7am–2pm and 4.30–9pm; free). The first entirely baroque building to be erected in Valencia, it is connected to the cathedral's dais by a high, enclosed bridge of Renaissance style used by members of the clergy only. The statue is poised on a swivel mechanism so that it can be brought to face the nave of the church or a small chapel intended for more intimate communion with the faithful. During Las Fallas she is honoured by a large display of flowers in the square outside the church.

Behind the church, through the arch formed by the bridge to the cathedral, is the Plaza Almoyna, site of the original Roman settlement of Valentia, off which are two lesser sights: an art gallery, the **Museo de la Ciudad** (Mon–Sat 10am–7pm, Sun 10am–2pm; free on Sun) housed in the former Palacio del Marqués de Campo, and **El Almudín**, a 13th–14th-century granary which once supplied the city with wheat and is now used to house exhibitions. Down an adjacent street, Calle del Almirante, is the only piece of Moorish architecture still standing in the city, the **Baños del Almirante** (Admiral's Baths; Tue–Fri 10am–6pm, Sat–Sun 9am–2pm; guided visits every half hour; free on Sun).

The other conspicuous building on the Plaza de la Virgen, set back from it slightly, is the seat of the Valencian regional government, the **Palau de la Generalitat** ❺. It looks old enough to be a fusion of Renaissance and Gothic, but only one tower is authentic – the other is a copy added in 1952.

CITY CENTRE

> ### 'Little Hunchback'
>
> The statue of Valencia's patroness Virgin is nicknamed the Geperudeta, the 'Little Hunchback', because of a curve in its back. The story goes that the statue assumed this form through use in the funeral rites of outcasts such as executed criminals. The sculpture would be laid on the corpse, her head resting on a cushion, a position that caused her 'curvature of the spine'.

Another important institution is housed in an old palace on the pedestranised Calle Navellos, which leads north from the Plaza de la Virgen towards the Torres de Serranos and the river. This is the **Cortes Valencianas** (Mon and Fri at 10, 11am, noon, and 1pm by appointment only, tel: 96 387 61 00; for details check www.cortsvalencianes.es; free), the regional parliament of the Comunidad Valenciana. It occupies the much-extended Palacio de Benicarló, which became the home of the Republican government in the Civil War after its exile from Madrid until the final victory of Franco's forces.

BARRIO DEL CARMEN

Take the street that runs beside the Palau de la Generalitat and you are on Calle Caballeros, the principal axis of Valencia's oldest and most atmospheric quarter, the **Barrio del Carmen** ❻, an organic network of narrow, erratically twisting streets and alleys which suddenly open out into unsuspected little squares, where you can sometimes hear the silence despite being in the heart of a modern city. For decades during the 20th century, this area was left to crumble into squalid, undesirable tenement housing; chunks of plaster were regularly dislodged from its discoloured walls by the ricochets of fireworks during the Fallas fiestas. Finally, however, the city council decided to rehabilitate it, allowing the area's unique character and the buildings' surviving architectural details to be enjoyed. At night it is transformed into one of Valencia's favourite nightlife haunts.

For a taste of the Barrio del Carmen you can just walk along **Calle Caballeros**, although this is not one of its typical streets because of the wealth of its residents. It is lined with mansions of more or less Gothic pedigree, mostly built around inner patios – which are often concealed behind street doors large enough to admit carriages when opened but forbidding enough to keep the riff-raff out when shut.

A better policy is to venture off this main street northwards. A right turn down Calle Salinas brings you to a curious example of how architecture can be adapted to new uses. A semicircular arch, the **Portal de Valldigna**, was once part of the 2-m (6.5-ft) thick wall built by Valencia's Muslim rulers and later used as a point of access to the medieval Christian city. In the 17th century, two houses on either side of the street were joined together over the top of the gate.

If you continue wandering in the same direction, you will come to the rectangular Plaza del Carmen, one of the oldest squares in the city, overlooked by the **Iglesia del Carmen**, founded in the 13th century and much altered since. It has a baroque façade on

Barrio del Carmen, a favourite nightlife haunt

Imposing Torres de Quart

three levels and an angel as a weathervane. The church once formed part of a Carmelite convent, which now contains the **Centro del Carmen**; Tue–Sun 11am–7pm; free), a cultural centre and museum displaying late-19th century to early-20th century Valencian art.

At the end of Calle Caballeros is the Plaza del Tossal. Here a section of the Moorish-era wall, together with a watchtower, can be seen in the **Galería del Tossal** (Tue–Sat 4–7pm, Sun 10am–2pm; charge). It is believed to be part of the al-Hanax gate, one of the city's five entrance points in the wall built between 1021 and 1061 when Valencia was capital of a Muslim kingdom.

A short walk beyond the Plaza del Tossal, down Calle de Quart, brings you to the edge of the Barrio del Carmen, marked by the **Torres de Quart** ❼, one of the old city gates. This was built between 1441 and 1460, using Naples' Castel Nuovo as a model. When the walls fell into disuse, the gate was turned into a women's prison. The holes that can be seen in the outside walls are said to have been made by projectiles fired by the French during their siege of Valencia in 1808 and left unrepaired as a memorial to the resilience of the citizens.

THE MARKET AND LA LONJA

South of the Barrio del Carmen, down Calle Bolsería from Plaza del Tossal, you come to three very different buildings sharing the triangular **Plaza del Mercado**, where those deemed heretics by the Inquisition were burned at the stake.

Church of the Sts John

The **Iglesia de los Santos Juanes** ❽ began life as a Gothic structure, built on the site of a mosque. It was badly damaged by fires in the 16th century and had to be almost totally rebuilt during the 17th and 18th centuries. Only the nave and a large blank disc at the west end, which was to have been a rose window, suggest the church's Gothic origins; otherwise it is a somewhat disappointing baroque. Still, the frescoes of the Apocalypse on the vaults by Antonio Palomino are worth seeing as are the statues of the Twelve Tribes of Israel, sculpted by Jacobo Bertessi.

The main façade, forming an odd juxtaposition with the other two buildings on the square, is unusual for having a terrace jutting out from its base which was used as a platform from which dignitaries could watch public spectacles.

> **Vane attempt**
>
> The spire of the Iglesia de los Santos Juanes used to be crowned by a weathervane of a bird which, according to tradition, was used as a distraction by poor parents who wanted to abandon their children: they would point to the bird and, when the child was looking up, slip away into the crowd.

Mercado Central

Below it are basement chambers with doors onto the street known as **les covetes de Sant Joan** (St John's caves). At the top of the façade is a clocktower with figures of the two St Johns to whom the church is dedicated.

Mercado Central

Adjacent to the church is the antidote to a morning spent sightseeing too many historical monuments: the **Mercado Central** ❾ (www.mercadocentralvalencia.es; Mon–Sat 7am–3pm). The principal market of the city, indeed one of the biggest markets in Europe, is housed in a handsome art-nouveau building with wrought-iron vaults and a central dome. Designed for the everyday business of buying and selling, it nevertheless has delightful ornamental touches in ceramic, brick and stained glass – most notably the red and yellow stripes of Valencia's flag, the *senyera*. When it was inaugurated in 1928 by King Alfonso XIII the market had well over 1,000 stalls. Consolidation among the traders has reduced this number to around 700, which still gives the shopper plenty of choice. The best time to get here is mid-morning when it bustles with people calling out their orders in Valencian and stuffing shopping baskets and trolleys with fruits and vegetables. If you are not going out into the *huerta*, where oranges are sold by growers by the roadsides, buy them here. Some stalls also sell herbs and spices, others dried fruit and nuts, and one specialises in ostrich eggs and meat. A separate part of the market is for fish and seafood.

Outside, if you are peckish, you can get some freshly fried *churros* – like long, thin doughnuts – a popular sweet snack, or a takeaway portion of paella. A stall near the entrance sells paella pans in a range of sizes with gas rings to match, together with the necessary cooking implements.

La Lonja

Across the road from the market is Valencia's favourite building, a true temple to commerce. **La Lonja** ❿ (Mon–Sat 10am–7pm, Sun 10am–2pm; charge), originally used for trading in silk and later as a general commodities exchange, is one of Europe's finest examples of civil Gothic architecture. It was modelled on a similar building in Palma de Mallorca and built between 1483 and 1498.

The exterior is lavishly decorated in carved stone with tracery, filigree, *ajimez* windows (divided into two lights by slender columns) and spiky crenellations beneath which gargoyles leap out. If you look closely at street level you can get a glimpse of the more playful side of the craftsmen responsible: among the figures incorporated in the stonework is one showing his naked buttocks to the observer.

The building is divided into three parts by a central tower, which contains a chapel and a prison once used for merchants who defaulted on their debts. The part to the left of the tower was occupied by two institutions: the **Consulado del Mar**, the regulatory body that oversaw maritime trade, and the **Taula de Canvis**, the city's first banking body, which was largely responsible for financing the construction of La Lonja.

Entering to the right of the tower, you step immediately into the building's most graceful space, the **Transactions Hall**, which is divided into three naves. The high ceiling is held aloft by eight gracefully spiralling columns which sprout at the top into stellar vaulting. An inscription running round the chamber reads, 'I am a famous house which took fifteen years to build. See how fine a thing commerce can be when its words are not deceitful, when it keeps its oaths and does not practise usury. The merchant who lives in such a way will have riches and enjoy eternal life.'

Behind La Lonja is a warren of narrow streets and squares dotted with small shops. With luck you should emerge underneath the tower of the Iglesia de Santa Catalina, at the corner of the Plaza de la Virgen, ready to visit a very different part of the city centre.

MUSEO DE CERÁMICA

From the bottom of Plaza de la Reina, a straight street, **Calle de la Paz**, leads towards the modern shopping zone of the city centre. Take the second turning on the left, Calle Marqués de Dos Aguas, to get to Spain's national ceramics museum, the **Museo Nacional de Cerámica González Martí** ⓫ (http://mnceramica.mcu.es; Tue–Sat 10am–2pm and 4–8pm; Sun 10am–2pm; charge). This is contained within an extraordinary building, the Churrigueresque (an extreme Spanish form of baroque) mansion of the Marquis of Dos Aguas: an 18th-century extravaganza of coloured plaster. The doorway is particularly striking. It is a dripping fantasy in alabaster designed by Hipólito Rovira and executed by the sculptor Ignacio Vergara. Ostensibly it is a portrait of the **Virgen del Rosario** but below it becomes a pun on the marquis' surname, Two Waters. On either side of the door two semi-nude male figures recline, while below them water representing the two rivers of Valencia, the Turia and Júcar, flows from twin pitchers. Around the figures runs a voluptuous mass of vegetation.

Beyond the portal, the museum doesn't disappoint. It is an eclectic delight of all things old and dazzling – even if you can't warm to pottery and porcelain, you are likely to find something to fascinate you. To begin with there are the rooms of the mansion itself, with their spiralling gold columns hung with grapes, cherubs and pink plaster cornices. They form the backdrop to everything on display. The most striking single exhibit, perhaps,

Interior of La Lonja, the 15th-century silk merchants' market

The Museo Nacional de Cerámica González Martí

is the marquis' Cinderella-style formal **Carriage of the Nymphs**, another Rovira/Vergara over-indulgence in excessive ornamentation. Other things to be seen include canopied beds and various items of furniture, a collection of Ex-Libris bookplates, old posters, photographs, books, sketches, engravings, caricatures, jewellery, silver and ephemera galore to do with celebrated Valencians.

The ceramics museum proper has some 5,000 pieces beginning with prehistoric, Greek and Roman specimens, passing through Oriental pieces, and ending with creations by Picasso. The core of it was amassed by Manuel González Marti, discoverer of potteries that flourished in the Middle Ages near Valencia. The outstanding treasures of the museum are medieval pieces made in ceramic-making towns near Valencia – Paterna, Manises and at the Royal Factory in Alcora – which are executed in greens, blacks and blues, often with metallic sheens. Among the more unusual pieces are 15th- and 16th-century examples of a technique associated with Paterna known as *socarrat* (between toasted and burnt). These tiles, which were designed to be placed between the beams on the ceiling, depict animals, flowers, ships, geometric patterns in spontaneous lines and rough shapes of red or black. The most popular exhibit in the museum is a complete traditional **19th-century Valencian**

kitchen richly decked out in ceramic tiles with panels depicting food and animals.

To see a more mundane use of ceramic decoration, continue down the street (it becomes Poeta Querol after the museum) until you come to the corner formed by the Teatro Principal. Look up left at the upper storeys of the neo-baroque 1935 triangular building of the **Banco de Valencia** building which forms a rounded corner between two streets. Above the penultimate balcony are two floors adorned with brightly coloured tilework against a contrasting red background.

THE UNIVERSITY AND EL PATRIARCA

The streets opposite the ceramics museum lead to two venerable Valencian institutions, the university and El Patriarca.

Colegio del Patriarca

CITY CENTRE

The neo-classical university was begun in the 15th century, although it is largely the result of later work.

Next to the university is the Real Colegio de Corpus Cristi, commonly known as the **Colegio del Patriarca** ⓬ (guided tours in English Mon–Fri at 11am and 5pm, Sat 11am; booking essential; http://patriarcavalencia.es; charge) in honour of its founder, the 16th-century archbishop and viceroy of Valencia, and Patriarch of Antioch, St John de Ribera (1532–1611). Ribera was a leading spirit of the Counter-Reformation, the repressive principles of which he applied in the seminary he founded. The focal point of the complex is a two-storey Renaissance patio composed of a double gallery of arches supported by 56 marble columns shipped in from Genoa. The statue in the middle of the courtyard depicts the archbishop himself, sculpted by local artist Mariano Benlliure.

To one side of the patio is a **church** whose walls and ceilings are entirely covered with richly coloured frescoes by Bartolomé Matarana. The 9.30am service (Tue–Sun and Thu 7.30pm) is in Gregorian chant. Above the altar you will normally see a beautiful version of the Last Supper by Francisco Ribalta, but during Friday morning mass (at 10.25) this is theatrically lowered to reveal a painting of the crucifixion by an anonymous 15th-century German artist hidden beneath.

There are various works of art scattered around the

The philosopher

In the patio of the university stands a statue of Valencian-born Juan Luis Vives (1492–1540), also known as Ludovicus. This brilliant philosopher and humanist spent most of his life outside Spain because of persecution due to his Jewish roots. In England he tutored Princess Mary (later Mary I) and took up a post at Oxford, where he formed close friendships with Thomas More and Erasmus.

Tranquil garden along the riverbed

Patriarca, including some fine Brussels tapestries. But several rooms are specifically dedicated to displaying an important collection of paintings by Spanish and foreign masters, including El Greco, Juan de Juanes, Caravaggio, Sariñena, Ribalta, Van der Weyden and Morales.

ALONG THE RIVER TURIA

It's not every city that can turn its river into a pedestrian urban freeway, but that is what Valencia has effectively done. After serious floods in 1957, the Turia was diverted through the outskirts to the south leaving its dry bed still flowing through the urban area in a large and strategic arc west to east. The bold decision was then taken to make the former course of the river into a ribbon of green for recreational use and the celebration of the arts, and it now serves as an elongated sports and cultural resource available to all, its amenities joined up by pedestrian and cycle routes.

For over 6km (4 miles), from the Puente Nou d'Octubre to the Puente de Astilleros, the riverbed is a procession of gardens, sports fields and playgrounds, all planted with a variety of trees, either native to the region or adapted to the climate, notable among them pines, palms, carobs and olives. Between these two crossing points are a further 17 bridges, seven of them expressly built as part of the riverbed rehabilitation project. If you want to walk the whole length of the river, begin at Nou d'Octubre station on metro line 3 in the suburb of Mislata (there are several buses that go there too).

THE UPPER TURIA

This river of gardens begins upstream in the west with the **Parque de Cabecera** (or **Capçalera**). Next to the park is the extraordinary **Bioparc**, an extensive zoo which recreates different African habitats.

The park is divided into several ecosystems: savannah, equatorial African forest, African wetlands and that of Madagascar. The African savannah includes an acacia forest and is inhabited by zebras, impalas, giraffes and rhinoceros. Big rocky formations recreate a typical African landscape, and lions rest on top of rocks overlooking the zebras and antelopes. There is also a palm forest inspired by those found in Kenya, and a stand of baobabs where a herd of African elephants can be seen drinking at the lake (opening hours vary, for details see www.bioparcvalencia.es; charge).

Next to this, on Calle Valencia, a continuation of the Passeig de Petchina (which runs along the southern riverbank), is the **Museo de Historia de Valencia** (Tue–Sat 10am–7pm, Sun 10am–2pm; www.museosymonumentosvalencia.com; charge),

The elephants are a highlight of the Bioparc

housed in a 19th-century water cistern. The exhibits tell the story of the city from its foundation by the Romans to the present day. Every section is equipped with a 'time machine', consisting of a life-size screen on which actors portray scenes from history in the language of your choice.

Follow the south bank of the river and on the other side of the Puente de Ademuz you'll find the **Museu Valencià d'Historia Natural** ⓭ (Natural History Museum; Sat–Sun 10am–1pm; www.mvhn.es; free). Behind this is the **Jardin Botánico** (daily 10am–6pm; closes 1–2 hours later in spring/summer; charge), a university botanic garden created on the present site – which was then outside the city walls – in 1802. It is planted with 4,500 species organised into 20 collections, including plants useful to humans, a tropical greenhouse, water plants, carnivorous plants, native Valencian species, woodlands and palms. Its most original feature is the Umbraculo, a pergola built of brick and iron.

A little further down the southern river bank, on the corner of Calle Guillem de Castro, is the **Instituto Valenciano de Arte Moderno** ⓮ (IVAM; www.ivam.es; Tue–Sun 11am–7.30pm, Fri until 9pm; guided visits by appointment; free on Sun and Fri from 7.30pm), which is considered one of the top modern art galleries in Spain. The collection concentrates on Julio

Torres de Serranos

González, acclaimed as the father of 20th-century Spanish sculpture. Its eight galleries include one in which remains of the medieval city wall can be seen.

If you prefer art at the opposite end of the chronological spectrum, have a look at the prehistory museum next to the IVAM, the **Museu de Prehistòria de València** ⓯ (Tue–Sun 10am–8pm; charge), in which you can see undeciphered engravings made by prehistoric people living in the hills of Valencia.

Round the bend in the river, just after Puente de San José, is a museum of art of a different kind, the **Casa Museo de José Benlliure** (Tue–Sat 10am–2pm and 3pm–7pm; Sun 10am–2pm; free on Sun). This is the former home of the prominent Valencian painter José Benlliure who died in 1937. There is a pretty garden with Valencian ceramics to wander round.

The next monument you come to, still on the same bank of the river, is the **Torres de Serranos** ⓰ (Mon–Sat 10am–7pm,

Sun 10am–2pm; charge). One of the few remaining bits of Valencia's medieval city walls – and more glamorous than the Torres de Quart – this gateway was built in the 14th century using one of the doors of Poblet monastery in Catalonia as a model and combines defensive and decorative features. Its two towers are topped by battlements as if ready for war, but the central panel over the gateway is embellished with delicate Gothic tracery, giving a clue that this is more triumphal arch than defensive installation. Its structure was left exposed at the back to prevent the towers being used against the citizenry. From the Plaza de los Fueros behind you can see its various chambers – which have cross-ribbed vaults – once used as a jail for miscreant nobles. Four gargoyles protrude from this rear wall.

Across the next bridge, the Pont de Fusta, is a railway station, once used for a quaint system of narrow-gauge railways but now serving the high-tech tram which departs for the beach. Down this next stretch of the northern bank of the river are two monumental buildings and two gardens. At the end of Puente de la Trinidad is the **Real Monasterio de la Santísima Trinidad** (guided visits only; book at http://monasteriotrinidad.es), a working convent inhabited by a closed order of nuns. The monastery door is pure Flamboyant Gothic.

Valencian artists

One part of the Fine Arts Museum of particular interest presents the work of three little-known Valencian artists of the 19th and 20th centuries who were inspired by the sea, the colours of the *huerta* and the light cast by the Mediterranean sunshine: Ignacio Pinazo, Antonio Muñoz Degrain and, above all, the Impressionist Joaquín Sorolla.

ALONG THE RIVER TURIA

> **Elio's mountains**
>
> Los Viveros occupies the site of a Moorish country house, later Christian palace and royal residence which was demolished during the Peninsular War. When the war was over, rubble from the palace was swept together to form two artificial hills, Las Montañitas de Elio, named after the general who ordered their building.

MUSEO DE BELLAS ARTES

Next to this is the **Museo de Bellas Artes** ⓱ (Museum of Fine Arts; Tue–Sun 10am–8pm; www.museobellasartesvalencia.gva.es; free) housed in a 17th-century seminary. This might not compete in size with the large galleries of Madrid and Barcelona but it has an important collection nonetheless, focusing on painting of the Gothic period. You enter via an octagonal vestibule covered by a blue cupola and ascend two floors of galleries. Upstairs, the most outstanding pieces are 'primitive' Valencian painting of the 14th and 15th centuries, represented by a series of huge golden altarpieces painted in tempera and later, under Flemish influence, in oils by artists such as Jacomart, Miguel Alcanyis, Maestro de Bonastre and Pere Nicolau. Other outstanding works include Hieronymus Bosch's *Triptych of the Passion*, showing the tormenting of Christ, and Velázquez's self-portrait. There are also works by El Greco, Van Dyck, Murillo, Ribalta and the local Renaissance painter, Juan de Juanes. There are six paintings by Goya here, although none of them is exceptional.

LOS VIVEROS AND BEYOND

The Museo de Bellas Artes stands at the corner of the city's largest garden, the Jardines del Real, better known locally as **Los Viveros** ⓲ (The Nurseries; daily 8am–sunset; free). The garden has a wide variety of different spaces within it connected by broad *paseos*. There are fountains, pergolas, a restaurant often used for weddings, lawns, ornately decorated benches, bronze and marble sculptures galore and a lake with ducks. Here and there are intriguing bits of historic architecture salvaged from demolition sites: a baroque doorway, a pink and grey marble fountain from a monastery, and sample houses from the Valencian *huerta*. The garden is the venue of popular concerts in summer and also includes the **Museo de Ciencias Naturales** (Natural Sciences Museum; Tue–Sun 10am–7pm; charge).

Near Los Viveros, a few steps away from the riverbed, are more gardens, this time protected from the rush and noise of the city by a wall. The **Jardines de Monforte** ⓳ were created in the 19th century by Juan Bautista Romero, a wealthy Valencian landowner, and designed by the architect of the bullring. They

Museo de Bellas Artes poster

are Italian in inspiration and neo-classical in style, with hedges closely trimmed into geometric forms, a long shady arbour, trickling fountains and a scattering of sculptures and marble statues, creating many intimate spaces.

From the corner of Los Viveros, the next kilometre of the left or north bank of the river becomes the Paseo de la Alameda, a broad avenue. Diagonally across the river from Los Viveros are two churches which would be worth seeing but are hard to visit: the **Iglesia del Temple**, which, as its name suggests, owes its origins to the Knights Templar, and the **Iglesia de Santo Domingo** (group visits only by appointment 8am–2pm; tel: 96 196 30 38), which has a beautiful Gothic cloister and 15th-century chapel but is now owned by the military.

Four bridges stand close to each other here, beginning with the stark white **Puente de Calatrava**. Built of extra-tensile steel and with a span of 131m (430ft) supported by a single arch set at 70 degrees from the horizontal, it was designed by the Valencian architect Santiago Calatrava, who is also responsible for the adjacent metro station (and most of the Ciutat de les Arts i les Ciènces).

On the city side of the river is the **Plaza Porta del Mar**, marking the site of the gate in the city wall that communicated with the harbour. This was the last gate to be closed at night and anyone absent-mindedly arriving late was forced to sleep in the open air across the river, giving rise to the expression 'to be left out under the moon of Valencia', meaning to be left in the lurch. These days

'La Peineta'

The sleek, white Puente de Calatrava has been given the nickname of 'La Peineta' for its resemblance to the ornamental combs worn by women as part of the traditional Valencian costume.

the term Luna de Valencia (Moon of Valencia) has been expropriated to refer to the city's nightlife.

A short way further down the river is the 10-arched **Puente del Mar**, built in 1591 and one of the oldest bridges still standing. Each end is marked by broad flights of steps and the bridge itself is adorned with canopied sculptures of the Virgin Mary and St Paschal.

Palau de la Música

Continuing down the riverbed parklands, the next sight you come to, beyond the Puente de Aragón, is the **Palau de la Música** [20], an ultra-modern concert hall which could almost be a greenhouse for the amount of glass incorporated into its remarkable construction. The main auditorium has such excellent acoustics that the Spanish tenor Plácido Domingo is said to have remarked after his first concert here that 'El Palau is a Stradivarius'. As well as ballet, opera, classical and jazz concerts, the Palau also hosts modern art exhibitions.

THE FINAL STRETCH

Over the other side of the next bridge, Puente del Angel Custodio, a giant sculpture of Jonathan Swift's **Gulliver** [21] lies prostrate in the riverbed acting as a great climbing frame and slide for children.

The last bridge before reaching the riverbed's end at the Ciutat de les Arts i les Ciènces is the city's longest. The **Puente**

del Reino marches obliquely across the river taking a nonchalant 220m (720ft) to get from one bank to the other and is lit by art-deco lampposts. Raised on plinths at either end are the guardians of the bridge: four snarling pseudo-Gothic gargoyles in bronze, human of body but with the heads of beasts and half-unfurled wings, designed by the engineer who built the bridge, Salvadór Monleón.

There is one more sight of interest on the south bank of the river, and that is the **Museo Fallero** on the corner of Plaza Monteolivete (Tue–Sat 10am–7pm, Sun until 2pm, free on Sun). The museum honours the tradition of the Fallas, the fireworks festivals held each year in March (see page 89), and houses *ninots*, comic figures in papier-mâché, which have been saved by popular acclaim from the usual conflagration.

THE CITY OF ARTS AND SCIENCES

As the bed of the River Turia nears the sea, the new developments along it reach a climax in the futuristic cultural

⊙ VISITING THE CITY OF ARTS AND SCIENCES

Except for the Oceanogràfic, it is possible to walk around the City of Arts and Sciences (www.cac.es) at your leisure and enjoy much of the architecture for free. If you want to visit all parts of it inside and out, however, you'll need to buy a combined ticket (€37.40 at the time of writing) giving admission to L'Hemisfèric, the Museu de Les Ciències Príncipe Felipe and L'Oceanogràfic. A ticket can be bought from any of the ticket offices or online. This is valid for one, two or three days (they don't have to be consecutive) and permits you to visit each attraction once only.

Zorbing in front of the Hemisfèric

complex of the **Ciutat de les Arts i les Ciències**, the City of Arts and Sciences. This ambitious complex aims to encourage visitors to combine leisure with an exploration of the arts, sciences and nature. It consists of five stunning, futuristic buildings, four of them by Santiago Calatrava, standing in a 1.8-km (1-mile) alignment.

PALAU DE LES ARTS

Approaching from the city, the first of the buildings is a spectacular concert hall, the **Palau de les Arts Reina Sofía** ㉒, which has a 75-m- (250-ft-) high, domed roof clad in white mosaic tiles. This was the last part of the complex to be completed. The building houses four separate theatres with a combined capacity of over 4,000 seats, designed to provide Valencia with a world-class stage for high-quality opera, concerts, ballet and theatre.

L'HEMISFÈRIC

The concert hall is separated from the other buildings by a bridge, the Puente de Monteolivete, on the other side of which is a hi-tech cinema, **L'Hemisfèric** ㉓, the first part of the city to open in 1998. This eye-shaped cinema has sides like folding portcullises which open and close in imitation of a blinking eyelid. Its singular aspect has been enhanced by placing it between two symmetrical shallow rectangular ponds. Under what turns out to be an elaborate oval canopy is a sphere stuffed with high technology where banks of comfortable seats look up at a gigantic, inclined, concave screen 24m (80ft) in diameter. The Hemisfèric's main function is to project the moving images of IMAX films which exceed the limits of human binocular vision, sucking the viewer into the larger-than-life action. It is an overwhelming sensory experience which can be dizzying and disorientating. The cinema is also geared up for laser shows and as a planetarium in which more than 9,000 stars are visible.

MUSEU DE LES CIÈNCIES PRÍNCIPE FELIPE

The next building is one of Spain's largest science museums, the **Museu de les Ciències Príncipe Felipe** ㉔ (Jul–Aug daily 10am–9pm, until 6pm in winter; charge), a sloping skeletal structure of steel and glass composed of vast intersecting white arches and taut buttresses. It looks like a cross between a cathedral, a space-age aircraft hangar, and the chalky skeleton of some fossilised sea creature.

The exhibitions are arranged on four floors, although you can walk about some parts of the building, notably Calle Mayor and the terrace, both one level up from the entrance, without paying the admission fee. The contents are fairly standard science museum exhibits, covering life, the Earth, science and technology with many interactive exhibits.

L'UMBRACLE

Opposite the science museum, across another shallow rectangular pond, is **L'Umbracle** (daily 8am–12.30am; charge). This is a cleverly disguised car park forming the south side of the complex and screening the rest of it from the road. The roof of the car park has been turned into a winter garden, covered by what looks like a giant white cloche – *umbracle* means arbour or pergola – 18m (60ft) high. If L'Umbracle is the least spectacular part of the city, it is also the most peaceful and a pleasant place to stroll around when you want to get away from the crowds. It is planted with various species of shrubs and trees native to Valencia and others selected for their adaptation to the climate. As the space has to make either an artistic or scientific contribution to the whole, there are several sculptures to admire in the shade, including *EX IT* by Yoko Ono.

L'Oceanogràfic, much more than an aquarium

L'OCEANOGRÀFIC

The final and largest part of the city is technically an aquarium but is, in reality, far more than that. **L'Oceanogràfic** (closing times are variable so check ahead at www.oceanografic.org; daily 10am–6–8pm, until midnight in summer; charge) is made up of a series of lagoons containing water varying according to salinity, temperature and depth to represent the five oceans, and various

> **Underwater dining**
>
> If you are truly in the aquatic mood, you may want to eat in one of L'Oceanogràfic's underwater restaurants, Submarino, where you will be served a seafood meal surrounded by swimming fish. Be warned, though, it quickly gets booked up and you will need to reserve your table as far in advance as you can (tel: 96 197 55 65).

pavilions or towers illustrating different marine environments – oceans, wetlands, tropical seas and the Arctic.

The last of these is an appealing igloo-like dome which is agreeably cool on a hot day outside. The whole place is connected by bridges, passageways and underwater glass tunnels – one being the longest such tunnel in the world.

Although it's certainly an imaginative juxtaposition of original architecture and wildlife, it could be said that there isn't enough of the latter to do justice to the former, even if the figures sound impressive: there are 10,000 individuals of 500 different marine species floating above, below or around you or, as is more usual in aquariums, sitting in dark corners of their tanks doing nothing. The whole place is conceived on three different levels and there are also a lot of ramps, stairs and lifts to negotiate as you go down into the depths to look at each habitat. Several events are staged during the day to add interest to a visit. The highlight of these is the dolphin and killer-whale show and it is worth making a note of the time of the next show when you arrive and getting to the dolphinarium early to save a seat.

THE SEAFRONT

Although much of Valencia's historical prosperity derived from its role as Mediterranean port, until recently the city always kept its distance from – and its back to – the sea. The urban centre grew up just over 3km (2 miles) from the coast, far enough for the harbour area, El Grau, to be thought of as a distinct, unsavoury haunt of sailors, poor fishermen and lowlifes. Even today, the inhabitants of the maritime quarters – mostly proud people with strong local traditions – speak of 'going to Valencia'. In the city centre, meanwhile, there is scarcely a hint of sea nearby except in the name of Avenida del Puerto, built at the start of the 20th century, leading discreetly off towards maritime perdition.

The relationship only started to change in the 1960s when new suburbs filled the void between the two parts of the city. But then came tourism, which made city planners realise that their seashore was something to develop rather than ignore. The shabby port was spruced up, a new promenade *(paseo marítimo)* built

The beach, overlooked by the port's cranes

for seaside recreation, and there were even controversial plans, eventually blocked by the Spanish Supreme Court, to continue Avenida Blasco Ibañez to the beach by bulldozing part of the historic Cabanyal fishing quarter. The final step in the rehabilitation of the seafront's reputation was the awarding of the 2007 America's Cup competition to Valencia (see page 12).

Now that the Avenida Blasco Ibañez extension isn't going ahead, there are still only two ways to see the sea. The most direct way is by bus or taxi down Avenida del Puerto, a straight street running from the Plaza Zaragoza. A more interesting trip is by tram from the Pont de Fusta station, across the riverbed from the Torres de Serranos; take metro line 4 in the direction of Doctor Lluch and get off at Les Arenes.

THE PORT

In preparation for the America's Cup, Valencia's port has been split neatly in two. The south side concerns itself with the container and passenger terminals (catering for trippers to and from Mallorca and Ibiza), while the wharves on the north side, adjacent to the beach, have been transformed into a marina and leisure complex which is pleasant to stroll around. This is also where the European Formula 1 Grand Prix was held until 2012; the circuit is now sadly rundown. Some of the more attractive parts of the old port have been retained on the side nearest the Avenida del Mar, including the handsome **Port Authority Building** with its distinctive clock tower and some warehouses in a restrained mercantile brand of art nouveau.

The new developments centre on a striking modern structure, the **Edificio Veles e Vents** ㉖ (Sails and Winds Building), an iconic water pavilion designed by UK architect David Chipperfield.

Set back from the harbour, next to the church of Santa María del Mar, is **Las Atarazanas** ㉗ (Plaza Juan Antonio Benlliure;

The handsome Port Authority building

Tue–Sat 10am–2pm and 3–7pm, Sun 10am–2pm; charge), an ensemble of five Gothic sheds built at the end of the 16th century to serve as a workshop for boat building, an arsenal and a place to store maritime tackle. At the time of their building they stood at the head of the beach. This is now used as an exhibition space.

THE PASEO DE NEPTUNO AND PASEO MARÍTIMO

Stepping out of the side entrance of the port brings you onto Valencia's flashy esplanade, the **Paseo Marítimo** ㉘, which begins with the pleasant **Paseo de Neptuno**. Along this little street are the front doors of a solid line of restaurants specialising in paella. Each has its back door opening onto the beach and almost all of them have glass-enclosed dining rooms and terraces. At weekends and in summer they can be very busy; at other times of the year you may well get the whole restaurant to yourself – but don't take this as an indication that the food is not good. Prices along

Cabanyal architecture

the restaurant strip vary and three establishments trade on ancient fame: La Pepica, L'Estimat and La Marcelina.

The Paseo de Neptuno ends abruptly at the luxury spa hotel of **Las Arenas** (or Les Arenes in Valencian), which retains two restored bright-blue classical temples (entirely rebuilt) that were once part of the old-fashioned restaurant complex that stood here.

From the corner of Las Arenas, the Paseo Marítimo becomes a 2-km (1.25-mile), palm-shaded multi-lane pedestrian motorway of dog walkers, pram pushers, joggers, ice-cream-licking toddlers and power-walking grannies. There is also a cycle track along the length of it. In summer the beach beside it can be packed with sunbathers, but off-season the fine golden sand provides a pitch for impromptu games of football or frisbee. The sea, except in exceptionally bad weather, has only a light swell, and is good for swimming: despite its proximity to a commercial port, most people consider it suitably clean.

For its last stretch, the Paseo Marítimo runs along **Calle Isabel de Villena**, where, in the late 19th and early 20th centuries, affluent Valencians built themselves fine holiday villas. Among these worthies was the novelist and sometime republican-leaning politician Vicente Blasco Ibáñez (1867–1928) who found inspiration from the uninterrupted views of the sea. His reconstructed house is open to the public as the **Casa-Museo Blasco Ibáñez** (Tue–Sat 10am–2pm and 3–7pm, Sun 10am–4pm; free on Sun), containing portraits, photographs and sculptures of the writer, books and memorabilia.

THE CABANYAL

A few streets back from the Paseo Marítimo is one of Valencia's best-kept secrets, the old fishing quarter of the **Cabanyal** ㉙. This was once a defiantly self-contained community where everyone knew everyone and fishermen would sit on the pavements outside their houses mending their nets. You can still see signs of this spirit in a few surviving family-run corner shops and neighbourhood bars, the best of which is the Casa Montaña, which was founded in 1836 (see page 109).

There are no museums or monuments of note in the Cabanyal. Instead, the charm is in the ordinary architecture, at least those examples which have survived successive attempts at modernisation. The Cabanyal grew up as a patchwork of *barracas*, typical Valencian houses with steeply pitched thatch roofs, that were aligned in long streets parallel to the beach so that fishing nets could be laid out to dry. Gradually, around the turn of the 19th and into the 20th century the *barracas* were replaced by small, low family homes which were less vulnerable to fire. Many of these were decorated by their owners on the outside in eclectic, highly idiosyncratic styles broadly inspired by *modernismo*, the Spanish version of art nouveau.

Easter week

The Easter week procession through the Cabanyal puts the rest of Valencia to shame with its ostentatious legions of participants dressed as Biblical characters, Roman soldiers and, strangely, Napoleonic grenadiers.

Several of the houses have façades entirely clad in colourful ceramic tiles, which reflect heat and humidity and keep the interiors cool. Others, especially near the seafront, are tastefully painted in one or two pastel shades. Everywhere there are playful details to admire: intricate ironwork ornaments, stucco motifs, a Phaoronic head on the tiles of a balcony, a frieze hinting at Moorish Spain, tulips rampant up a door jamb, gargoyles and grotesque heads peering over the street. Look for them on any of the old streets: Reina, Barraca, Padre Luis Navarro, José Benlliure or Escalante.

Almost all the old houses in the Cabanyal are low level, of human proportions; many are back-to-backs and some are so small that they have only one room upstairs and one downstairs. The entire neighbourhood of Cabanyal is undergoing a thorough redevelopment with old houses being renovated, pavements widened and streets realigned. In 2017 alone more than €36 million has been allocated to upgrade the area.

AROUND THE CITY

Valencia's hinterland is easily explored by car or public transport from the city centre. You have a choice of fertile farmland, a watery nature reserve, historic ceramics-making centres or a medieval monastery.

THE HUERTA

If it is possible to visit Valencia without being reminded of the proximity of the sea, it isn't easy to come away ignorant of the existence of an intensely fertile agricultural plain surrounding the city. Valencians have an almost spiritual attachment to this prime piece of farmland, the *huerta*. From its produce their city originally grew wealthy; later it was relied on to help them

The highly cultivated huerta

survive through hard times; and today the *huerta* continues to fill markets and provide the raw materials for Valencia's traditional dishes and drinks.

Yet this natural resource is under threat from modernity. Theoretically, the *huerta* extends over a semicircle of land roughly bordered by the River Júcar to the south and the hills that start around Sagunt in the north. In practice, however, it is shrinking rapidly as it is encroached on by the growth of dormitory towns and the inexorable expansion of the outskirts of the metropolis.

But there is still *huerta* left and in places you can get an idea of how it must have looked in the days when agriculture was a leading industry here. At its most perfect, close to the city, the *huerta* is composed of smallholdings where not even the smallest patch of land is allowed to go to waste. The fine soil beneath the immaculate rows of artichokes, tomatoes, aubergines and flowers looks

Oranges are Valencia's major export crop

as if it has been sifted, fed and spoiled for generations, which it undoubtedly has. Given the warm climate, these plots can produce up to four crops a year if they are worked with care.

Such high productivity, of course, depends upon water. Crucial to farming the *huerta* are the *acequias* (irrigation channels) whose use and misuse is argued over weekly by the members of the Water Tribunal (see page 33). On its arrival at Valencia, the River Turia is checked by an ingenious system of dams, sluices and overflows which feeds eight principal *acequias* in proportion to the amount of land they supply. These and other less noble *acequias* criss-cross the *huerta*, branching into ever smaller divisions to form a watery labyrinth of glistening channels. The original irrigation system was probably devised by the Romans, but it is the Moors who are credited with perfecting it; they came from Syria, Lebanon and Egypt where they knew all about the importance of irrigation to farming.

That the *huerta* has made fortunes for some enterprising farmers can be seen in the proud, exotic farmhouses, *alquerias*, that poke out from among the foliage. Some of them have towers and fanciful oriental touches; many have ceramic ornamentation gleaming in the sun. Much less common are *barracas*: traditional peasant houses with steeply pitched thatched roofs.

LA ALBUFERA

One corner of the *huerta*, **Alboraya** ③⓪ has built its fortune by specialising in a particular crop, the *chufa* or earth almond, *Cyperus esculentus*, a brilliant green, spiky, grass-like plant which is thought to have been introduced by the Moors. When the tubers of this plant are mashed with water and sugar they become *horchata*, a sweet milky drink which is served cold in summer (see page 103). The *chufas* of Valencia have their own *denominación de origen*, like wine grapes.

Another plant introduced to Spain by the Moors is the orange, which has since become Valencia's most famous export crop.

When the trees flower in late February to early March the sweet smell of the blossom – *azahar* – fills the air and even pervades the built-up areas. String bags of ripe oranges hung on sale by the side of the road or next to a front door are a common sight in the first few months of the year. When buying oranges, don't be put off by their often blotchy or scarred appearance. These unattractive fruit, rejected by wholesale export buyers, have plenty of juice and an intense flavour. The tastiest oranges, it is said, remain in Valencia.

LA ALBUFERA

To the south of the city, where there is even more water available, the *huerta* becomes a checkerboard of paddy fields which are sown and flooded in the

Barraca in La Albufera

Ploughing the rice fields

spring for the rice to mature over the summer. In July and August the leaves of the crop reach full height and the whole area flushes a vivid emerald green. Over winter, after the autumn harvest, the landscape turns into a watery maze.

The rice fields converge on **La Albufera** ③, a freshwater lake beside the coast which is one of the Iberian Peninsula's prime wetlands for birds and easily reached from Valencia by the motorway to El Saler. The lake is fed by the River Turia and connected to the sea by three channels or *golas* which are fitted with sluice gates to control the water level. It is extremely shallow, up to only 2.5m (8ft) deep, and is gradually shrinking because of natural silting and the reclamation of land by rice farmers. In the Middle Ages the lake was 10 times its present size.

If your main interest is primarily wildlife you may want to go first to **Raco de l'Olla** (by the turn-off to El Palmar), where there is an information centre (daily 9am–2pm; tel: 96 386 80

50; free) with a glass-domed observation tower for birdwatching. On the other hand if you are more interested in food, the village of **El Palmar** is the authentic place to eat paella and *all i pebre* (eels cooked with garlic and pepper). El Palmar is also the departure point for boat trips around parts of the lake.

If you are feeling adventurous you can try to negotiate the tracks that lead around the edges of the rice fields and along irrigation channels south from El Palmar to the low hill of **La Muntanyeta de Sants** and, eventually, the N332 main road.

La Albufera is separated from the sea by a strip of sand dunes and Mediterranean woodland, 10km (6 miles) long and 1km (0.5 mile) wide, called the **Dehesa** which is fringed with sandy beaches, making it popular with tourists. When the beach-lovers have gone home it is a good place to take an evening stroll.

CERAMICS TOWNS

Manises 32, next to Valencia's airport, has been synonymous with ceramics since the Moors introduced the craft. The **Museo de Cerámica de Manises** (Tue–Sat 10am–1.30pm and 4–7pm, Sun 11am–2pm; free) has a permanent exhibition of

⊘ BIRDS OF LA ALBUFERA

Well over 300 species of bird have been recorded in La Albufera, a figure which includes vagrants making a one-off appearance. With patience and binoculars you are usually sure to see herons (night, squacco and purple), egrets (cattle and little), ducks, waders, terns and gulls. Shy species like the bittern make good use of the lake's reed beds and marshy islands, *matas*, to hide in. The bird population spills over into the neighbouring rice fields in search of food.

El Puig Monastery

2,500 pieces dating from the 14th century to the present day. It's worth taking a stroll around the old town to browse in the ceramics shops and to see some beautiful tiled façades and colourful door jambs.

There are more ceramics in **Tavernes Blanques**, a short way north of the city, where the Lladró company has its factory and the **Centro Cultural y Museo Lladró** (Mon–Fri 9.30–6pm, Sat 9am–2pm; free). Visitors see the whole process from design to the kiln, together with an exhibition of current and past products. The Lladró brothers' art collection – including works by El Greco, Sorolla, Zubarán Ribera and other Spanish artists – is on display in a separate hall.

EL PUIG MONASTERY

About 15km (9 miles) north of Valencia is the Mercedarian **Real Monasterio del Puig de Santa Maria** ㉝ (Tue–Sat 10am–noon and

4–5pm, Sun at noon, beginning on the hour; visit by guided tour only, book by calling 96 147 02 00 or e-mail mercedariospuig@gmail.com; charge). In 1237, on the eve of the conquest of Valencia by the forces of King Jaime I, a statue of the Virgin Mary was found on a hill on this spot. A church was built to house the statue, which was adopted as the patroness of the new Christian kingdom. In 1588 the church gave way to the monastery, a forbidding rectangular building with four stout corner towers. The guided visit takes you through two cloisters and into the refectory, chapel, hall and other rooms where there are numerous works of art.

In one wing is the **Museo de la Imprenta y de la Obra Gráfica** (Museum of Printing and Graphic Arts), which has a facsimile of what is thought to be the first book printed in Spain: *Les Obres o Trobes en Lahors a la Verge Maria*, printed in Valencia in 1474.

EXCURSIONS

Many varied but little-known places are within reach of the city of Valencia, especially if you have hired a car – although most can be reached with public transport. The easiest to get to are on the coast, or at least on the coastal plain. The nearest of them are still in Valencia province, but rewarding one- or two-day excursions can be made northwards to the Costa del Azahar, the coast of Castellón province, and south towards Alicante and the Costa Blanca. Below are the nearest and most worthwhile destinations for a day out.

SAGUNT

In 219BC, Saguntum, a Roman outpost on the Via Augusta whose foundation long predates Valencia, was sacked by the Carthaginian general Hannibal, an attack which was to spark the Second Punic War and lead to the subjugation of Spain by Rome. Among other monuments, the Romans built a theatre on the hillside above the present-day town of **Sagunt** ㉞ (30km/18.5 miles north of Valencia by road or rail), exploiting a natural hollow for its acoustic effects.

In 1896 this theatre was the first building in Spain to be declared a national monument. In the 1980s the decision was taken to rehabilitate it for contemporary performances of drama and music, but the restoration work made controversial use of new materials and techniques and not everyone has been happy with the result.

On the crest of the hill above is a sprawling **castle**, which from the 5th century BC was the site of the Iberian settlement of Arse. Over the centuries it was added to by successive civilisations. Almost 1km (0.5 mile) in length, it is divided into seven plazas or divisions. There are beautiful views from it over the town and the sea. (The castle and Roman theatre are open Tue–Sat 10am–6pm, till 8pm in summer, Sun 10am–2pm; free.)

Below the theatre and castle, the core of the **old town** is medieval, set around the porticoed main square. The most atmospheric part is the old Jewish quarter, which is laid out in irregular narrow streets and passageways.

PEÑÍSCOLA

In the extreme north of Castellón province is the old fortified town of **Peñíscola** (140km/87 miles north of Valencia on the A7 motorway), built on a rocky promontory into the sea. Its castle, the **Castell del Papa Luna**, erected on the foundations of a Moorish fortress, is mainly the work of the Knights Templar and their cross can be seen carved above the door. It later became the residence of the papal pretender Pedro de Luna, cardinal of Aragón, who was elected Pope Benedict XIII during

Peñíscola, viewed from the Knights Templar castle

the Great Schism that split the Christian Church at the end of the 14th century. He retired here after he had been deposed and died a nonagenarian in 1423 still proclaiming his right to the papacy. The castle was used as a location for the film *El Cid*. Beneath the castle walls is a delightful labyrinth of steep, narrow cobbled streets lined with white houses, enclosed by massive ramparts and entered by two gates.

To the north of the old town is an immensely long, straight sandy beach stretching to the next resort of Benicarló. There is also a smaller curve of beach to the south, next to the harbour.

GANDÍA

The Duchy of **Gandía** ❸ (65km/40 miles south of Valencia by the A7 motorway) was bought by one Rodrigo Borja in 1485. As Pope Alexander VI he founded the clan known better by the Italian spelling of its name, Borgia. He himself is

The built-up beach at Gandía

remembered for his scandalous private life, but his illegitimate son, Cesare, and daughter, Lucrezia, have become definitions of debauchery. The family's reputation was redeemed by Alexander's great-grandson, who was born in Gandía in 1510 and canonised in 1671 as St Francis Borgia. Following the death of his wife, he turned his back on the pleasures of the world, joined the Society of Jesus (the Jesuits) and devoted himself to spreading the ideas of the Counter-Reformation.

For all his saintly work he remained a nobleman and his birthplace, the **Palacio Ducal** (Duke's Palace; Mon–Sat 10am–1.30pm and 3–6.30pm in winter, Mon–Sat 10am–1.30pm and 4–7.30pm in summer, Sun 10am–1.30pm; www.palauducal.com; charge), is an opulent building inside, even if no hint of this is given by the simple Gothic courtyard you enter by. The interior decoration, with its painted ceilings and gilded doorways, reaches a zenith in the baroque Golden Gallery, commissioned by the 10th duke of Gandía to celebrate his ancestor's canonisation. One room on the tour has a concentric circular tiled floor made in Manises representing the four elements of earth, air, fire and water. Gandía has some beautiful sandy beaches and is known for its typical dish, *fideuà*, a kind of paella made with vermicelli instead of rice (see page 101).

XÀTIVA (JÁTIVA)

You can follow the Borgia line backwards by going inland from Gandía to **Xàtiva** ❸❻ (60km/37 miles southwest of Valencia), the birthplace of the two popes who founded the clan. The Phoenecians are thought to have first settled the site. In the 11th century, Europe's first paper was made in Xàtiva by the Moors out of rice and straw. A huge ribbon of a **castle** (Tue–Sun 10am–7pm, closes 6pm in winter; www.xativa turismo.com/castell-de-xativa/; free on Tue afternoon), with 30 towers, once the most important fortress under the Crown of Aragón, runs along the ridge above the town. On the way up to the castle are two very old chapels: the 13th-century **San Feliu** (St Felix; Tue–Sat 10am–1pm and 3–6pm in winter; 10am–1pm and 4–7pm in summer, Sun 10am–1pm), which has a Romanesque doorway, pink marble columns and paintings from the 14th and 15th centuries, and **San José** (Tue–Sat 10am–1pm and 3–4pm, Sun 10am–1pm), which has a viewpoint outside it.

Among the sights in the narrow streets and small squares of the old part of the town are a former hospital with a

> ### ⊘ THE UPSIDE-DOWN KING
>
> Xàtiva was a prosperous place until, as part of the kingdom of Valencia, it backed the losing side in the War of the Spanish Succession, that of Archduke Charles of Austria. Retribution followed the Battle of Almansa in 1707, when the victor, Felipe V, burnt down the town and renamed it San Felipe. In the 19th century, the city fathers reclaimed the old Moorish name and exacted their revenge by hanging Felipe's portrait upside down in the municipal museum – and that's the way it has remained.

> **Raisin' the roof**
>
> Many of the older houses in the countryside surrounding Jávea have an unusual feature testifying to the local land use: a *riu-rau*, an arched stone porch where grapes were hung to dry into raisins in the circulating air.

Plateresque façade (opposite the 16th-century collegiate church), and a medieval fountain in Plaça de la Trinidad. The municipal museum Museo del Almodí (Tue–Fri 10am–2pm and 4–6pm; Sat–Sun 10am–2pm; free on Sun), meanwhile, has an unusual royal portrait in its collection.

DENIA AND JÁVEA (XÀBIA)

The two closest resorts of the Costa Blanca to Valencia are Denia (100km/62 miles south by the A7 motorway) and Jávea (10km/6 miles further), separated by the humpbacked hill and nature reserve of Mount Montgó (753m/2,470ft). They are very different in character from each other and between them offer a range of beaches.

The bigger and busier of the two is **Denia**, which was founded as a Greek colony and named after the goddess Diana. For a while in the Middle Ages it was the capital of a Moorish kingdom and the oldest parts of its **castle** date from that time. North of the harbour, past the old fishermen's quarter, is the long, wide sandy beach of Las Marinas; to the south is the more discreet and rocky Las Rotas, which has some good snorkelling. In the first two weeks of July Denia holds its Toros a la Mar festival, a bull-run up to the water's edge.

Jávea, over the hill, is in two parts. Its town centre is perched on a hill a short way inland, on the site of an Iberian settlement. Many of the buildings lining the streets – including the town hall and cinema – are made from the local characteristic tosca sandstone. The 16th-century church of **San Bartolomé** is an imposing piece of work as it was fortified to serve its congregation as a refuge in times of invasion. Over the door are machicolations through which missiles would be dropped on to attackers.

Most buildings around the port and main beach, which are overlooked by a line of ruined 17th- and 18th-century windmills, are modern but relatively low-level as a result of council policy to keep Jávea from being dominated by the high-rise apartment blocks seen in other resorts.

The rest of Jávea's shoreline is rocky. Pirates and smugglers once took advantage of the hiding places afforded by the cliffs, caves and inlets between the lighthouse at Cape San Antonio and Granadella Cove.

Jávea cove

Corpus Christi celebration

WHAT TO DO

SHOPPING

Valencia is a pleasant city in which to shop. If it lacks the specialist or chic retail outlets of Madrid and Barcelona, at least it isn't overwhelming in its variety. It has a good balance between small, old-fashioned family-run shops and ultra-modern shopping centres. Plus it has the advantage that you can get around most of the shops on foot.

Although manufacturing has declined in favour of service industries, Valencia still offers a few traditional specialities that make good souvenirs: ceramics is its main craft, but locally made leather and wooden goods (guitars, castanets, pipes), fans and, most practical of all, paella pans are all available.

WHERE TO LOOK

The modern shopping streets of Valencia lie roughly within an area bounded by the busy streets of Colón, San Vicente Mártir, Játiva and Calle de la Paz. They include Don Juan de Austria, Barcas, Roger de Lauria and Correos. All these streets are within an easy walk of the Plaza del Ayuntamiento. The shopping continues down Jorge Juan and around the Mercado de Colón and along the Gran Vía Marqués del Turia. Traditional craft shops are around the cathedral area and behind the Lonja.

DEPARTMENT STORES AND SHOPPING CENTRES

A good one-stop shop for just about anything is **El Corte Inglés** department store (www.elcorteingles.es), which has four branches that all stay open at lunchtime. The main ones are Pintor Sorolla 26 (on the corner of Jardines del Parterre, at the end of Calle de la Paz) for fashion, and Calle Colón 27 for everything else, including books and recorded music.

The closest shopping centres to the city centre, all filled with national and international chain stores, are **Nuevo Centro** (which has a branch of Corte Inglés; www.nuevocentro.es), across the riverbed **El Saler** (www.elsaler.com), opposite the City of Arts and Sciences, and the Gran Turia centre (http://es.club-onlyou.com/Gran-Turia) on Plaza de Europa.

MARKETS AND STREET MARKETS

The **Mercado Central** (open Mon–Sat 7am–3pm; www.mercadocentralvalencia.es) is a tourist attraction in itself, and the art-nouveau **Mercado de Colón** (open 8am–1.30am; www.mercadocolon.es) is also a delight. But for a real feel of the city visit a neighbourhood market such as the **Mercado Ruzafa** (Mon–Sat 7am–3pm; http://mercatderussafa.com) or the **Mercado del Cabanyal** (Mon–Sat 7am–2.30pm, until 8.30pm on Fri; www.mercadocabanyal.es), near the seafront.

There is a street market every day of the week in one part of the city or another, with stalls selling cut-price clothes and household items. The most important are in **Calle Convento Jerusalén** on Tuesdays, **El Cabanyal** (around the market) on Thursdays and **Benicalap** on Saturdays. Sundays is fleamarket *(rastro)* day around the **Plaza Redonda** where a bit of everything, including books, plants and animals, is on display.

FASHION

The best places to look for designer labels and jewellery are calles Colón, Sorní, Cirilo Amorós, Jorge Juan and Ensanche. The most expensive shops are in this area. **Loewe** has a shop at Marqués de Dos Aguas 7 (for women) and **Louis Vuitton** at Carrer del Poeta Querol 5. The Spanish fashion designer **Adolfo Dominguez** has a shop at Hernán Cortés 12. Nearby, in Calle Colón, are two Spanish chains with more affordable prices, **Zara** and **Mango**.

CERAMICS AND OTHER CRAFTS

The best place to shop for ceramics is Manises, but there are a number of good shops in the centre of the city where you'll find a range of household items and ornaments. Try, for instance, **Cobalto y Cobre** (Plaza Redonda; www.cobaltoycobre.es) or **Artesanía Colla Monlleó** (Plaza Redonda 12). Also in Plaza Redonda, **Chez Ramón** sells handmade ceramics and wrought-iron lamps. Nearby, at Plaza Milagro de Mocaoret 5, a tiny square through an arch from Plaza de la Reina, is **Yuste** which sells ceramics, crafts and custom-made items. **Lladró**, the world-famous porcelain manufacture, has a shop at Poeta Querol 9, facing the ceramics museum.

Traditional Spanish fans – very practical for hot, summer days – have been made near Valencia since the 15th century. You will find a wide variety of fans at a range of prices in **Nela** (Calle San Vicente 2, near Plaza de la Virgen). However, the best place to shop for them is, without doubt, **Abanicos Carbonell** (Carrer de Castelló 21, tel: 96 341 53 95; www.abanicoscarbonell.com), a family business which has been going

Pottery stall in Plaza de la Reina

Craft shop on Plaza Redonda

since 1810 and is run by a fourth-generation master fan-maker who will show you his collection of 18th- to 21st-century fans on request. Some fans are less functional accessories than *objets d'art*, each one the work of perhaps 20 different craftsmen.

Other crafts shops are **Huerta de San Vicente** (San Vicente Mártir 41; https://huertasanvicente.com), which sells craftwork from Andalucía and the rest of Spain; and, for jewellery, **Argimiro Aguilar** (Calle Colón 41; www.argimirojoyero.com).

FINE FOOD AND WINE

Any large supermarket will stock a range of Valencian and Spanish products. However, the best place to go for fresh produce and spices – and for a spot of people-watching – is without doubt the **Mercado Central**.

For wines not available in supermarkets, there are several high-class specialist wine shops. These also double as delicatessens, selling fine cheeses, hams, olive oils, *turrón* (a traditional Spanish nougat eaten at Christmas) and other gourmet Spanish products. **Bodega Baltasar Seguí** (Poeta Emilio Baró, 17) is family-owned and of long pedigree.

Most *pastelerías* have a good choice of sweet things to try. There are sweet shops in Calle Muro de Santa Ana, beside the

Torres de Serranos. **Trufas Martinez** (www.trufasmartinez.com) at Calle Ruzafa 12 sells delicious chocolate truffles.

PAELLA PANS

If you are inspired to go home and cook your own paella, you'll need the proper pan to do it, and possibly a cooking support for it or gas ring – it is important that heat reaches all of the pan evenly. Paella pans come in a range of sizes, from tiny to enormous, and they are classed according to how many people they will serve. The easiest place to find them is outside the **Mercado Central**. You can buy the ingredients inside the market at the same time.

⊙ THE LANGUAGE OF THE FAN

Hand-operated air-conditioner, fashion statement, art canvas and even advertising hoarding, the Spanish fan served and continues to serve many functions but none more successfully than that of text messenger. In the days when young men and women were forbidden to talk to each other directly without going through a chaperone, a language of fans evolved so that from a distance ladies were able to communicate their desires and arrange trysts from balconies or behind grilles or across ballrooms without anyone else knowing what was being said. There was even an alphabetical fan code which enabled words to be spelled out letter by letter, though due to its complexity it was rarely used. Those in the mating game, however, would be in no doubt as to the meaning of a fan wafted across the heart (I love you), a half-open fan held over the face (they're watching us!) or the holding up of the fan to shield the face from the sun (you're ugly!).

Paprika for sale at the Mercado Central

FURNITURE AND ANTIQUES

Valencia holds an international furniture trade fair every year and has a wide range of shops in Sedavi, Alfafar, Benetuser and Beniparrell. For classic and avant-garde furniture, try **La Oca** at Cirilo Amorós 38; www.laoca.com.

Calle Músico Peydrò (parallel with San Vicente Mártir) is known for its wicker, cane, bamboo and pine furniture and ornaments. Shops include **Cestería el Globo** (www.cesteriaelglobo.com) at No. 16.

Antiques shops and dealers are concentrated in the old town in streets such as Avellanas, Baja and Purisima.

ENTERTAINMENT

During the city's frequent fiestas you won't be short of entertainment. There's plenty to do the rest of the year, whether your taste is for a formal concert or a casual night of bar-hopping. To find out what's on in Valencia see the weekly listings magazine *Cartelera Turia* (www.carteleraturia.com), available from newsstands.

MUSIC

The principal venues for performances of classical music, opera and ballet are the **Palau de la Música** (Paseo de la Alameda 30, tel: 96 337 50 20; www.palaudevalencia.com) and the four halls in the **Palau de les Arts** (tel: 96 197 58 00 or 902 202 383; www.lesarts.com; see page 57), which is located in the City of Arts and Sciences.

Rock, pop, jazz and blues are more often to be found in more intimate venues such as the **Black Note Club** (Polo and Peyrolón 15, tel: 96 393 36 63; www.blacknoteclub.com).

THEATRE AND CINEMA

Most theatrical performances are in Spanish or Valencian, although occasionally international companies do perform. The main theatre is **Teatro Principal** (Barcas 15, tel: 963 539 200 for tickets; http://teatres.gva.es).

Almost all films, whether shown at the cinema or on television, are dubbed into Spanish, but **Filmoteca Generalitat Valenciana** (IVAC, Plaza del Ayuntamiento 17, tel: 96 353 93 00) and **Babel** (Calle Vicente Sancho Tello 10, tel: 963 626 795; www.cinesalbatrosbabel.com) often show foreign films in their original language with subtitles (look for 'VO' – *version original* – on posters). Most cinemas have three or four showings a day from 4pm to 11pm. Every October Valencia hosts an international festival of film, showcasing films from the countries around the Mediterranean; http://mostraviva.org/wordpress/?lang=en.

NIGHTLIFE

Valencia is well known for its nightlife – the so-called Luna de Valencia (Moon of Valencia) – nurtured by its benign outdoor climate. Most of the action is in bars called *pubs* which are not at all like their British namesakes: in Spain, *pubs* have minimalist décor, loud music and few seats. They don't open until late – the young rarely begin a night out before

> **La madrugada**
>
> The prime nightlife time, the small hours of the morning from midnight to daylight, is called *la madrugada*. It comes from the Spanish word, *madrugar*, meaning to get up very early.

11pm – and stay open till the early hours. Most *pubs* won't close before 3am and discos before 5am.

Broadly, Valencia's nightlife can be divided into four zones. The **Barrio del Carmen** is said to be favoured by bohemians, and offers some historical atmosphere to enjoy between drinks. Two well-known bars are **Café Negrito** (on Plaza del Negrito) and **Bolsería** (Calle Bolsería 41).

The bars around the Plaza Cánovas del Castillo, on the Gran Via Marqués del Turia are upmarket and the haunt of the city's rich kids. The two other pleasure zones along Calle Juan Lorens (near the Mercado de Abastos) and the avenidas of Aragón and Blasco Ibañez, and the Plaza de Xúquer are in the modern parts of town. For an altogether more elegant – and expensive – night out there is the **Juan Carlos I Marina** with its elegant seafront bars open throughout the night.

Gays and lesbians have their own night-time haunts. Starting points for men could be the restaurants with floor shows **Pekado** (Plaza Vicente Iborra 9 in the Barrio del Carmen; www.pekado.com) and **Turangalila** (Av. Maestro Rodrigo 13; www.turangalila.es), and for women **Mogambo** (Sangre 9), beside the city hall.

FIESTAS

Spanish fiestas have to be seen to be believed, and Valencia does them particularly well. Most are inspired by a religious pretext, although sometimes this is not readily apparent. If you do find yourself here during a fiesta, forget about doing everything else except enjoying it: streets are likely to be cut off, some shops and museums closed and restaurants and public transport full – but there will not be a dull moment.

LAS FALLAS

The big fiesta of the year in Valencia is Las Fallas, from 12 to 19 March. It's very noisy but also very spectacular, and if you want to know Valencia you have to see it at least once. Hotels are usually fully booked months in advance. The fiesta supposedly originated in medieval times when the city's carpenters would burn their rubbish in the streets outside their workshops on the arrival of spring.

The first week of March, in the lead-up to Las Fallas, there are great processions of people in traditional costume and a *mascletà* – a daylight firework display – in the Plaza del Ayuntamiento every day at 2pm. Then from 12 March until the end it is noise and commotion all the way. There are concerts in the streets, paella-making competitions, bullfights and people letting off fireworks whenever they feel like it.

On the night of 15–16 March hundreds of *fallas* are put in place throughout

During Las Fallas, a giant flower sculpture of the Virgen de los Desamparados is displayed on Plaza de la Virgen

Fallas take up to a year to make

the city. Each *falla* – which may be up to 25m (80ft) high – is a set-piece sculpture making a satirical point; figures called *ninots* form mini-scenes within the *falla*. Teams of artists take a whole year to design and build the wood, papier-mâché and fibre-glass figures. To see as many *fallas* as possible, go to a newsstand for a copy of *El Turista Fallero*, which includes a map. The best *fallas* are classed as *sección especial*.

The days of 17 and 18 March are dedicated to the patroness of Valencia, the Virgen de los Desamparados, and a giant floral sculpture of her is made in the Plaza de la Virgen. On the night of the 18th there is a firework display in the riverbed. The climax of Las Fallas occurs at midnight on the 19th, when the *fallas* are filled with fireworks and set alight one by one. Last to go up in flames is the biggest *falla* of all, the one in the Plaza del Ayuntamiento, in front of the city hall.

EASTER WEEK (SEMANA SANTA)

The fishing quarter of El Cabanyal stages colourful processions from Palm Sunday to Easter Sunday. Around 5,000 people, organised into 27 *cofradias* or brotherhoods, take part. Many of them dress as Biblical characters while others appear as Roman soldiers or, anachronistically, in the uniforms of Napoleonic grenadiers.

The best processions to see are the Silent Procession at midnight on Maundy Thursday and the slow, solemn Procession of the Burial of Christ on Good Friday, which starts around 6pm. The Procession of the Resurrection on Easter Sunday is a more joyful affair, during which the participants throw flowers to the spectators.

CORPUS CHRISTI

The Corpus Christi parade (on a date between mid-May and mid-June, depending on the date of Easter) sets off in the late afternoon to the sound of the *tabalet* (drum) and *dolçaina* (a kind of flute) and does a circuit of the streets in the old part of the city around the cathedral. It is essentially an ecclesiastical parade centring upon the great monstrance that is normally kept in the cathedral museum, but the whole occasion is surrounded by colourful traditions. Over 270 people take part as costumed Biblical personalities, giants, *cabezudos* (carnival figures with overlarge heads), eagle-people and *cirialots* who carry tall candles. In the

⊙ THE FALLAS MAKERS

If Las Fallas seems like a waste of otherwise good pieces of art (and money), consider this: which other city is able to generate an endless supply of work for its artists? A permanent colony of them are kept busy in the 60 workshops of the Ciutat Fallera in Benicalap, knowing whatever wonderful creations they dream up and take a year to painstakingly build will be reduced to ashes the following 19 March. Fortunately, a handful of *ninots*, the comic figures that populate the *fallas*, are saved from the flames by a vote each year and placed on display in the Museo Fallero (see page 56).

midst of all of them is la Moma, a person dressed in white with the face covered by a Venetian mask, who symbolises virtue victoriously resisting the seven deadly sins who dance around him or her. An essential part of the procession are the 10 *rocas*, mobile stages on which mystery plays were once performed.

JULY FAIR (FERIA DE JULIO)

This summer celebration has nothing to do with religion and everything to do with livening up the city during a month when citizens are tempted to abandon it for the country or the beach – at least that was the rationale for the 19thcentury city council to create it. Most events take place in the Paseo de la Alameda and in the Viveros garden. They include fireworks; rock, pop and jazz concerts; theatre; ballet; and a brass-band competition. There is also a calendar of first-class bullfights in the bullring. The climax, on the last Sunday of the month, is a battle of flowers in the Alameda: an hour of gentle carnation throwing.

SPORTS

SPECTATOR SPORTS

The great spectator sport in Valencia is **football**. The city's internationally successful team, Valencia CF, plays at the Campo del Mestalla, in Avenida de Suecia (tel: 00 34 902 01 19 19), a stadium with a seating capacity of 49,000. Valencia's other team is Levante UD.

Bullfighting takes place at the Plaça de Bous (Plaza de Toros; tel: 902 10 77 77), near the main railway station. If you want to see a fight it is best to go with someone who can explain what is going on and to be prepared for what you see: the ritualised killing of animals in an unequal fight. Tickets can be surprisingly expensive and get booked up quickly for important *corridas*. Cheaper seats are in the sun *(sol)*; the more expensive in the shade *(sombra)*.

Cheste, due west of Valencia on the Madrid road, has a **motorcycle** racing circuit. **Cycling** competitions take place at the Velódromo Luis Puig; **basketball** is played in the Pabellón Fuente de San Luis.

Valencia has an excellent basketball team

PARTICIPANT SPORTS

The **parklands** of the Turia riverbed are available year-round for anyone who wants to jog, cycle, rollerblade, skateboard, practise athletics or play football. Another good place for jogging or cycling is the Paseo Maritimo beside the beach.

For **swimming** there are Valencia's beaches and an open air pool in the Parque del Oeste in summer and the indoor swimming pool at the Complejo Patraix (c/Azagador de las Monjas 10; www.complejopatraix.com) in winter. For **horse riding**, contact La Hípica at Calle Jaca 23 (tel: 96 361 53 63; www.lahipica.com). **Tennis** players can practise at the University Campus of Universitat de Valencia (Menéndez and Pelayo 19, tel: 96 398 32 36). The Real Club Náutico de Valencia (Camino del Canal 91, www.rcnv.es) coordinates **yachting** activities.

There are six **golf** courses within Valencia province. The closest to the city is Campo de Golf de El Saler (Los Pinares, El Saler, tel: 902 54 79 79; www.parador.es), which has been ranked as

Terra Mitica ride

one of the 50 best golf courses in the world. Other courses near the city are those of El Bosque, Manises and Escorpión.

VALENCIA FOR CHILDREN

Children are universally welcomed in Spain at any time of day or night. There are, however, seldom special allowances or facilities for them such as high chairs and children's portions in restaurants, but waiters and other staff will generally go out of their way to help.

If hiking around the monuments of the city is not for your children, a compromise may be to take a ride on the Bus Turistic or in a horse-drawn carriage, both departing from the Plaza de la Reina. Some sights may please both adults and kids. The obvious ones are the **City of Arts and Sciences**, especially **L'Hemisfèric** IMAX cinema and **L'Oceanogràfic** with its shows of performing dolphins, and the **Bioparc** at the **Parque de Cabecera**. A surprisingly child-friendly museum is the **Museo de Historia de Valencia**, which has life-size display screens. The bed of the River Turia has lots of space to play, and a giant climbing frame-cum-slide in the shape of Gulliver is near the Puente del Angel Custodio.

A kids' treat for a long day out from Valencia is a visit to **Terra Mitica** theme park near Benidorm (tel: 902 020 220, www.terramiticapark.com), around an hour and a half each way by motorway.

CALENDAR OF EVENTS

5 January Cabalgata de Los Reyes – parade in honour of the Three Kings who arrive on this day bringing children their Christmas presents.
17 January St Antony's Day – pets and other animals are taken to be blessed by a priest on a podium in Calle Sagunto.
22 January Procession in honour of St Vincent the Deacon, co-patron of the city.
12–19 March Las Fallas – festival culminates on 19 March with the ceremonial burning of giant figures.
Semana Santa (Easter week) Processions in the Cabanyal.
San Vicente Ferrer (Sunday and Monday after Easter) Children act out the miracles of St Vincent Ferrer on a stage set up near his birthplace at the end of Calle de la Mar.
May Fiesta de La Virgen de los Desamparados (second Sunday in May) – festival in honour of Valencia's patroness; a statue of the Virgin is carried in procession from her basilica to the cathedral.
May or June Corpus Christi procession takes place in the streets of the old city around the cathedral.
23–24 June Fiesta de San Juan (St John's Night) – with bonfires on the beach.
July (all month) Feria de Julio – July Fair, ending with the battle of the flowers on the last Sunday.
August (last Wednesday) La Tomatina – a battle with tomatoes in the town of Buñol, west of Valencia; (last Sunday) La Cordá – a spectacular firework festival in Paterna outside Valencia.
September (first week) Grape harvest festival in the wine-growing region of Requeña.
9 October Fiesta de la Comunitat Valenciana – commemoration of the reconquest of Valencia in 1238 by Christian forces with a procession carrying the regional flag leaving from the city hall.
Mid-October Mediterranean Film Festival.
1 November Día de Todos Los Santos (All Saints' Day/Day of the Dead) – people decorate the city's cemeteries with flowers.

EATING OUT

Eating out is one of the great pleasures of a visit to Valencia. Not only does the city have a huge range of fresh produce but also the climate to make it possible to have a meal outdoors for much of the year.

The city's numerous restaurants range in atmosphere from laid-back to formal. Dishes native to other parts of Spain can be sampled, but most restaurants describe themselves as offering Valencian cuisine which, as much as referring to a number of emblematic, rice-based dishes, effectively means making optimum use of the freshest of ingredients available at the local market, fish and seafood being foremost among them.

MEALTIMES

Mediterranean Spain's eating hours vary greatly from those of the rest of Europe. For many visitors, the late mealtimes can take some getting used to. Breakfast *(desayuno)* is of little importance. Many Spaniards will have only a light meal first thing in the morning – a few biscuits or a piece of toast with a milky coffee, or perhaps a glass of fresh orange juice in a bar. They save their appetites for a proper breakfast mid-morning, around 10.30 or 11am. It is at this time you will see bars and cafés packed with people tucking into a sandwich or piece of toast for *almuerzo*.

The city's shops and offices close at around 1 or 1.30pm (which to the Spanish is midday) and the bars fill up again, this time for tapas and a beer or wine. First-time visitors are often alarmed at how long Spaniards put off lunch (*la comida*), the main meal of the day – most restaurants won't even open until 1.30pm and will not start filling up until well after 2pm. It is considered acceptable to sit down for a meal at 3.30pm, a time

Dishing up paella

when the rest of Europe is halfway through the afternoon. The Spanish, of course, consider that everyone else in Europe eats too early, and they claim that their late lunchtime allows them to get a full morning's work done.

Anyone who has the opportunity will prolong lunch over coffee, and perhaps brandy and a cigar, and then put their feet up for the *sobremesa*, the lazy digestion time after lunch or even have a siesta, especially if it is a hot day in summer.

At 4 or 5pm the afternoon (*la tarde*) begins. Many people fill the long haul between lunch and dinner with a visit to a café or a *pastelería*, at 6 or 7pm, for something sweet. This stop-gap meal is called *la merienda*.

Some foreign visitors feel they are wasting away by the time restaurants open for dinner/supper (*la cena*). Only those places geared up for tourists will be open before 8pm. Around 9pm is a more usual time to dine, and many locals may not even sit down to dinner until after 10pm. However, there are plenty of bars in Valencia where you can eat tapas, and fast-food restaurants open for long hours without a break in the middle of the day.

PAELLA

Valencia's speciality is paella, Spain's most famous dish. It is eaten wherever the occasion presents itself, but although there are take-away versions for eating in the streets it is usually kept as a semi-special treat for an office outing or as a way to bring the family together on a weekend. It is at its best when it forms part of a leisurely lunch (never dinner) with friends: it is a meal to share and the dish itself can be a good icebreaker for conversations.

An ingenious combination of ingredients which can look as good as it tastes, paella originated as a simple dish that the labourers of the *huerta* could prepare over an open fire during the rice harvest using one shallow, round pan. The first paellas were flavoured with eels – abundant in the wetlands around the Albufera – and eaten communally, straight from the dish, each person with a wooden spoon working his way through an allotted segment,

◉ PAELLA ETIQUETTE

Don't trust any restaurant that offers you an instant paella; proper paella is a dish that needs to be served as soon as it is cooked. You will normally be asked to order at least half an hour in advance, stating how many people it is for (usually a minimum of two). As you finish your appetisers the paella will be brought to your table for your approval and served in front of you. It is best eaten with a squirt of lemon and no accompaniments, except a salad and a pitcher of beer or bottle of wine. Don't be afraid to use your fingers to attack the chunks of meat.

courteously respecting his neighbours' portions.

Over time, the checklist of ingredients for a good paella resolved itself into the recipe for the *paella valenciana*. As well as rice, a truly authentic paella is made with chicken, rabbit and snails – although you can consider the last item as optional.

Purists will allow a *paella marinera*, made from seafood instead of meat, but they regard with abhorrence the so-called *paella mixta*, combining the two in the same dish.

Calamares a la romana make a great starter

The two principal vegetables in paella are *bajoqueta* (green beans) and *garrofó* (a large, pale butter bean). Two other beans – *ferraura* and *tavella* – are sometimes used as well, and artichokes are added by some chefs. Rosemary lends its distinctive perfume to the simmering rice, as does saffron, which also turns the rice yellow. Nowadays, almost everyone below gourmet level substitutes cheap artificial colouring for the expensive saffron and the dish comes out tasting just as good.

No other ingredients are needed. Peas, tomatoes, peppers, garlic, sausages and the million and one other 'improvements' that slip into bogus paellas across Spain and in foreign countries have no place in the genuine article. They seldom enhance the appearance of the dish and they certainly create a confusion of tastes.

Paella is cooked in a particular kind of metal pan (widely available in Valencia in a variety of sizes), by preference over a wood fire but in practice usually over a gas ring. The important thing is for the pan to be level and the heat evenly distributed from centre to rim. Although there are recipes to follow, it takes the skill and intuition of an experienced cook to add the right amount of stock and let it simmer over an even heat, just long enough for the paella to reach the table with the rice cooked to the point of tenderness, neither dry and crunchy, nor moist and mushy. Really good paellas even have a light layer of delicious semi-burnt crust beneath the rice, called *socarrat*, which has to be scraped off the bottom of the pan: paella afficionados consider this a delicacy.

OTHER LOCAL SPECIALITIES

Paella is not the only thing on a Valencian menu, it should be emphasised; Valencia excels at rice dishes in general. One of the most popular after paella is *arroz a banda*, rice cooked in fish stock. This was originally a way of using tasty but bone-ridden fish which were trapped in nets and not worth the fuss of eating individually. In restaurants nowadays, good-quality fish is used for the dish, and this will be served separate to the rice, accompanied by *all i oli*, a garlic-flavoured mayonnaise.

Arroz al horno (*arros al forn* in Valencian) has an altogether different taste, being an oven-baked dish made with chick peas, pork, potato, sausage, tomato, garlic and black pudding. In the days before domestic ovens, housewives would prepare this dish in an

Churros

A favourite Spanish snack, eaten mostly in winter, is *chocolate con churros*: thick hot drinking chocolate into which is dunked sugared, deep-fried batter sticks (*churros*).

Arroz al horno, another delicious rice-based dish

earthenware casserole and take it to the local baker's to have it cooked. Yet another variation on the theme of rice is *arros negre* (black rice), which is made with squid, the ink giving the dish its colour and name.

If you want a change from rice, in the La Safor region around Gandía they make *fideuà*, a kind of seafood paella in which the rice is replaced with vermicelli. In the Albufera, look on the menu for *all i pebre d'anguiles* – a stew made with eels, garlic and paprika. Another typical Valencian dish, perhaps more modest, is the cold salad, *esgarrat*, made with red peppers, dried salt cod and olive oil.

As for sweets, Valencians are expert in turning almonds into all things delicious. *Turrón* (nougat) and *mazapanes* (marzipan), favourite Christmas treats, are made in Alicante, inland from the Costa Blanca. The town of Casinos, in the hills northwest of Valencia, is known for its *peladillas* – whole almonds covered in

Al fresco lunch

sugar. Other delights to be found in *pastelerías* (cake shops) are *rollitos de anis* (aniseed-flavoured biscuits), *rosegones* (small, hard almond biscuits), *pasteles de boniato* (pies of sweet yam) and *susus*, sticky doughnuts filled with a creamy custard. At Easter, soft and subtly sweet *panquemado*, literally 'burnt bread' but in reality something akin to brioche, makes a good breakfast or goes well with an afternoon coffee.

TAPAS

Tapas are little, appetizing snacks ordered at the bar to accompany a glass of wine or beer – Spaniards will rarely be seen drinking without eating something to go with it. Because tapas are available all day, they are a good way to fill gaps between meals or, if you order enough of them, to replace a meal altogether. But be careful: although it seems like an inexpensive way to eat, you can easily run up a larger bill than expected and pay more for an evening of tapas than you would have done for a *menú del día* (set menu). It's cheaper, by the way, to eat at the bar than to have a seat at a table.

There is rarely a tapas menu that can be brought to the table to study. Some items may be chalked up on a board or else the barman or waiter will reel off a long list of them and, if you are lucky, explain what they are. The simplest thing is to point to anything you fancy displayed on the counter. If you are stumped, all bars everywhere will serve you a wedge of *tortilla de patata* (potato omelette), a scoop of marinaded olives or a few slices of cheese (*queso*) or *jamón serrano* (cured ham).

If you want something more substantial than a tapa, ask for the same dish as a *ración*, which is always at least double the size of a tapa and often much more. You can also ask for an in-between quantity, a *media ración*. Almost anything that can be served as a tapa can just as easily be put into a baguette to make a *bocadillo* (sandwich) to eat in or take away.

WINE AND OTHER DRINKS

Valencian vineyards are generally not well known outside the region, but they are gradually making a reputation for themselves. Those of Utiel and Requeña, the main growing areas, produce some good rosés and medium-strength dry reds. The cold continental climate of Valencia's Alto Turia district, meanwhile, favours dry white wines.

If you bar-hop your way around Valencia, you'll almost certainly come across something a little stronger: Agua de Valencia, a cocktail of sparkling wine, orange juice and vodka which slips down all too easily.

If you prefer something non-alcoholic, Alboraya, just outside Valencia, is the birthplace of a refreshing summer drink popular all over Spain, *horchata*, a sweet milky drink made

Horchata is made from crushed tiger nuts

from crushed tubers (called tiger nuts). In the city centre, the best place to try it is Santa Catalina, a *horchatería* off Plaza de la Reina, but the best place to drink it is in Alboraya, specifically in the *horchatería* Daniel (www.horchateria-daniel.es). *Horchata* is always served cold and you can ask for it as a liquid *(liquida)* or semi-frozen *(granizada)*. You can drink it straight or copy the locals and dunk soft sweet cake sticks *(fartons)* or crunchy breadsticks *(rosquilletas)* into it. Although you can now buy packaged *horchata* all year round in supermarkets, it is not comparable to the fresh product. Another drink served by cafés and *horchaterías* is *leche merengada*, a kind of milkshake with egg and sugar added and flavoured with lemon and cinnamon.

Horchata-making often goes with ice cream and Valencia has a reputation in Spain for producing the country's best ice creams, a skill supposedly derived from its historical connections with Italy.

TO HELP YOU ORDER

Could we have a table? **¿Nos puede dar una mesa, por favor?**
Do you have a set menu? **¿Tiene un menú del día?**
I'd like a/an/some… **Quisiera…**
The bill please **La cuenta, por favor (El compte, per favor)**

MENU READER

agua water
al ajillo in garlic
a la plancha grilled
al punto medium
arroz rice
asado roasted
atún tuna
azúcar sugar
bacalao salt cod
bocadillo sandwich
boquerones anchovies
bien hecho well done
buey/res beef
calamares squid
cangrejo crab
caracoles snails
cerdo pork
cerveza beer
champiñones mushrooms
chorizo spicy sausage
cocido stew
cordero lamb
ensalada salad

entremeses hors-d'oeuvre
gambas prawns
helado ice cream
jamón serrano cured ham
judías beans
langosta lobster
leche milk
mariscos shellfish
mejillones mussels
pan bread
patatas potatoes
pescado fish
picante spicy
poco hecho rare
pollo chicken
postre dessert
pulpitos baby octopus
queso cheese
ternera veal
tortilla omelette
verduras vegetables
vino wine

EATING OUT

PLACES TO EAT

We have used the following symbols to give an idea of the price for a three-course meal for one, including wine, cover and service:

€€€€ over 60 euros
€€€ 30–60 euros
€€ 20–30 euros
€ below 20 euros

CITY CENTRE

Restaurants

Ana Eva € *Turia 49, tel: 96 391 53 69, www.restauranteanaeva.es.* Ana Eva serves good, inexpensive vegan cuisine in informal surroundings near the Torres de Quart. For starters try the *ensalada silvestre* made with beansprouts and mixed varieties of lettuce, for main course mushrooms with tofu in a basil sauce, and for dessert crème caramel made with carob flour. Closed Mon–Sunday.

Joaquín Schmidt €€€ *Visitación 7, tel: 96 340 17 10, www.joaquin schmidt.com.* Chef Joaquín Schmidt Río-Valle has created a very personal restaurant, somewhere between cutting edge and classic but still charming and intimate. There's a very good wine list, and the service is impeccable. Choose between three set menus of varying sizes and prices. The largest, and most expensive, the 'Joaquín Schmidt Menu', allows you to sample seven dishes, as well as cheese and dessert. The frequently changing lunch menu is less expensive. You can also book cooking classes with the Chef. Closed Monday lunch and Sunday.

La Carme €–€€ *Pl. de Mossén Sorell 7, tel: 96 392 25 32.* Tue–Sat 9–11pm; Sat–Sun 2–4pm. A no-nonsense, inexpensive place to eat in the Barrio del Carmen. The three-course menu allows little choice, but all the food is freshly prepared with a touch of imagination. Closed Monday.

La Riuà €€ *Calle de la Mar 27, tel: 96 391 45 71;* www.lariua.com. La Riuà has been serving home cooking by a husband and wife team since 1982. Their Valencian cuisine includes a wide range of rice, fish and shellfish dishes, and the restaurant is acclaimed for its paella, and other rice dishes, *fideua* and *all i pebre*. Book in advance at this legendary restaurant. Closed Sunday night and Monday.

Ricard Camarena €€€€ *Av. de Burjassot 54, Bombas Gens Centre d'Art, tel: 34 963 35 54 18,* www.ricardcamarena.com. This Michelin-star restaurant owned by one of Spain's rising chefs, Ricard Camarena, has a modern, minimalistic, albeit cozy, wooden interior. It offers a fusion of typical Valencian flavours and cutting-edge culinary art. A short daily menu includes plenty of fresh regional Mediterranean ingredients including seafood, vegetables and rice all prepared in the most creative way. Book well in advance. Closed Mon.

Seu Xerea €–€€ *Calle Conde de Almodóvar 4, tel: 96 392 40 00,* www.seuxerea.com. A meeting of Mediterranean, British and Oriental cuisines in a slick restaurant not far from the Plaza de la Virgen. Starters might include mussels in green curry or Thai-style fishcakes, while mains might be tuna in teriyaki sauce or slow-roast lamb with cumin sauce; finish with a coconut sorbet. At lunchtimes there is a cheap *menú del día*. Much more pricey is the excellent *menú de degustación* (taster menu). Open Tue–Sat 1.30–3.30pm; 8.30–11pm.

Taberna Alkazar €€€ *Mosén Femades 9 and 11 (Zona Peatonal), tel: 96 352 95 75,* www.tabernaalkazar.com. The Alkazar is an upmarket seafood and paella restaurant that first opened its doors in 1950. Choose a table inside or outdoors in the pedestrianised street. There's a busy tapas bar if you don't feel like a full meal. Large selection of wines. Weekdays 10am–midnight, from 11.30am Sat–Sun.

Tapas bars

Note: it is difficult to give a guide price for bars as the bill will vary enormously according to what you order.

100 Montaditos € *Plaza de la Reina 10, tel: 96 391 92 27*; http://spain.100 montaditos.com. One of a chain serving inexpensive tapas, especially, as the name says, 100 different kinds of open sandwiches or *montaditos*.

El Pilar € *Moro Zeit 13, tel: 96 391 04 97*. One of the oldest tapas bars in the city, dating from 1912, and as famous as ever for its mussels.

ALONG THE RIVER

A Tu Gusto €–€€ *Escritor Rafael Ferreras (on the corner with Avenida Instituto Obrero), tel: 636 557 476*, www.atugusto.com. Relaxed place a few streets away from the City of Arts and Sciences where you can enjoy creative Mediterranean dishes and a very good value lunch-time menu. Closed Mon.

El Colmado de la Rivera €€ *Calle Rivera 14, tel: 96 381 97 01*; http://el colmadodelariveravalencia.com. Conveniently located opposite Plaza de Toros, 'El Colmado de la Rivera' serves arguably the best squid in town. Other specialities include a great variety of exquisite tapas and paella made upon order. A reasonably priced *menú del día* is good value for money. Open daily 11am–1am.

Marisquerías Civera €€€ *Mosén Femandes 10, tel: 96 352 97 64*, www.marisqueriascivera.com. Fish and seafood restaurant of long standing in the historic centre of the city. Apart from the seafood, there are also some meat and vegetarian options. Open daily for lunch and dinner.

Submarino €€€ *L'Oceanogràfic, City of Arts and Sciences, tel: 96 197 55 65*, www.restaurantesubmarino.es. Relatives of the fish on your plate swim around you at this novelty underwater restaurant at the L'Oceanogràfic aquarium. Rice dishes are also served. Reservation is essential.

THE SEAFRONT

Restaurants

La Paz €€ *Paseo Neptuno 68, tel: 96 356 19 83*; www.restaurantelapaz.es. Splendid location with sea view makes it one of the best places to have paella and seafood dishes. Daily menu is a perfect budget option. Daily noon–5pm.

La Pepica €€€ *Paseo Neptuno 6, tel: 96 371 03 66,* www.lapepica.com. A classic Valencian restaurant founded in 1898 and visited by Ernest Hemingway and other writers, as well as bullfighters, artists and assorted VIPs. It is situated on a street along the beach which is lined with paella restaurants – some cheaper and where, arguably, you can eat just as well. La Pepica is known not only for its rice dishes but also for its lobster stew and grilled fish. Try the speciality of the house *Paella Pepica*. Daily lunch, Fri–Sat dinner.

La Rosa €€–€€€ *Paseo Neptuno 70, tel: 96 371 20 76.* Not as well-known as La Pepica, this is another good place to eat paella while watching the waves at sea. Also good for fish and seafood. Good wine list.

La Sucursal €€€€ *Muelle de la Aduana, tel: 96 374 66 65,* www.restaurantelasucursal.com. A Michelin star restaurant offers not only the very best of Valencian haut cuisine but also splendid views over marina and the surrounding area. Mon–Fri lunch and dinner, Sat–Sun dinner only.

L'Estimat €€–€€€ *Paseo de Neptuno, 16, tel: 96 371 10 18;* www.restaurante-cocinamediterranea.com. You can eat gazing out to sea in this restaurant, which is one of the more traditional ones on the Playa de las Arenas beach. It has been serving paellas and other rice dishes since 1927. Closed Tue.

Taj Mahal €–€€ *Doctor Candela 20, tel: 96 330 62 64,* http://restauranteindiotajmahal.com. This Indian/Pakistani restaurant, decorated with handicrafts and paintings, is in the suburbs between the city and the seafront (between Avenida del Puerto and Avenida Blasco Ibáñez). All the spices are imported from the Indian subcontinent. Open daily lunch and dinner.

Tapas bars

Casa Montaña €€ *José Benlliure 69, tel: 96 367 23 14,* www.emilianobodega.com. This tapas bar, which was founded in 1836, has been turned into a tasting centre for fine wines. Around a thousand types from around the world, but especially Valencia, can be ordered by the glass. All the dishes on the menu are made from carefully selected ingredients and include mussels, grilled sardines, squid, anchovies, typical Cabañal recipes, codfish croquettes, and different Spanish cheeses and cold meats. Open daily, only lunch on Sunday and holidays.

OUTSKIRTS

Alquería Del Pi €€–€€€ *Camino Viejo de Godella 55, tel: 96 365 17 70, www.alqueriadelpi.com*. A traditional Valencian farmhouse of the *huerta* standing in a 19th-century Mediterranean garden. Off a small road heading north out of the city.

El Rek €€ *Pintor Martí Girbés 1, El Palmar, tel: 96 162 02 97, www.elrek.com*. El Rek is located outside the town of El Palmar, in the heart of Valencia's rice-growing area and beside La Albufera. The menu consists of traditional Valencian cuisine, including *paella*, *arroz a banda* and *arroz negro*. The restaurant has its own landing stage for boat trips around the lake. Wed–Sun 1–5pm.

La Matandeta €€€ *Carretera Alfafar–El Saler km 4, Alfafar (7km/4.5 miles from Valencia), tel: 96 211 21 84, www.lamatandeta.es*. Fresh fish and seafood are served in a typical country house in the *huerta*. Here paella is cooked over an open wood fire, which gives the dish a delicious smoky flavour. Wed–Sun 10am–5pm.

Raco' Nou €€€ *Carretera de El Palmar 21, El Palmar tel: 96 162 01 72, www.nouraco.com*. Typical Valencian cuisine at this long-established restaurant – including rice dishes, seafood and *all i pebre* – served beside La Albufera. Set menu options start from €33 per person.

BUNOL

Venta Pilar €–€€ *Avenida Pérez Galdós 5, tel: 96 250 09 23*. At around 300 years old, this former staging post turned hotel-restaurant serves simple, homemade food. The daily menu offers excellent value compared with the more expensive à la carte options. The dishes, which include local as well as Spanish specialities, can be served in one of the dining rooms or at the outdoor patio. Try one of its wonderful, smoky rice plates prepared over an open fire. There is also a 1960s-style café which does breakfast and lunch.

CULLERA

Casa Salvador €€€ *L'Estany de Cullera, tel: 96 172 01 36*, www.casasalvador.com. Casa Salvador is in two *barracas* (typical Valencian farmhouses) next to a freshwater lake used for fish farming. It is a family business which claims to have been open every day for the last 50 years. Choose from a wide range of rice and fish and other typical Valencian dishes, including *arroz negro* and whole fish baked in a salt crust. There's an outdoor terrace overlooking the lake. Open daily 1–5pm and 9pm–midnight.

DENIA

Quique Dacosta Restaurante €€€–€€€€ *Urbanización El Poblet, Carretera Les Marines 3km, tel: 96 578 41 79*, http://quiquedacosta.es. This three-Michelin star restaurant is famous for its innovative take on Mediterranean cuisine. The DNA the Search menu pays homage to regional culinary traditions while being blended with the chef's boundless imagination and creativity. Wed–Sun lunch and dinner. Booking essential.

GANDIA

Telero €€ *Calle Sant Ponc, 7 Bajo, tel: 96 286 73 18*, www.telero.es. Friendly atmosphere and excellent service make this homely restaurant a perfect place to try traditional Valencian cuisine. The rice dishes and tuna steak are highly commendable. Vegetarian and gluten-free dishes also available. Good choice of regional wines. Closed Sun.

PENISCOLA

Casa Jaime €€€ *Avenida Papa Luna 5, tel: 96 448 00 30*, http://xn--casajaimepeiscola-pxb.com. The menu is mainly strong on rice dishes and fresh fish from the coast of Castellón. Fine selection of home-made desserts. Closed Wednesday in winter.

SAGUNT

La Mandorla €€–€€€ *Subida al Castillo 44, tel: 96 266 43 82*, www.larmeler.com. Arguably one of Sagunt's best restaurants is in the old Jewish quarter, on the way up out of the old town towards the Roman theatre and the castle. It serves excellent Italian cuisine with dishes on the menu including pizzas, risottos, meats and tasty steak tartar. Daily 6pm–midnight.

XATIVA

Casa La Abuela €€–€€€ *Calle Reina 17, tel: 96 227 05 25*. 'Grandmother's House' has changed over its 50-year existence from a simple restaurant into an establishment renowned for its cooking, still based on traditional local recipes, particularly Valencian rice dishes. Excellent *arroz al horno* is worth a try. Closed Wed–Sun night.

A–Z TRAVEL TIPS

A SUMMARY OF PRACTICAL INFORMATION

- **A** Accommodation _____ 114
  - Airports _____ 114
- **B** Beaches _____ 115
  - Bicycle hire _____ 115
  - Budgeting for your trip _____ 116
- **C** Camping _____ 117
  - Car hire _____ 117
  - Climate _____ 118
  - Clothing _____ 118
  - Crime and safety _____ 118
- **D** Driving _____ 119
- **E** Electricity _____ 121
  - Embassies and consulates _____ 121
  - Emergencies _____ 122
- **G** Getting there _____ 123
  - Guides and tours _____ 124
- **H** Health and medical care _____ 124
- **L** Language _____ 126
- Lost property _____ 126
- **M** Maps _____ 127
  - Media _____ 127
  - Money _____ 128
- **O** Opening times _____ 129
- **P** Photography _____ 129
  - Police _____ 130
  - Post offices _____ 130
  - Public holidays _____ 131
- **R** Religion _____ 131
- **T** Telephones _____ 132
  - Time zones _____ 132
  - Tipping _____ 133
  - Toilets _____ 133
  - Tourist information _____ 133
  - Transport _____ 134
- **V** Visas and entry requirements _____ 135
- **W** Websites and internet access _____ 136
- **Y** Youth hostels _____ 136

A

ACCOMMODATION (see also Recommended hotels on page 137)
Spanish hotels are awarded one to five stars according to their facilities – a system that tells you nothing about quality, views or the history of the building, let alone intrinsic personality. Hostels (*hostales*, denoted by the letter H outside) and *pensiones* (boarding houses, denoted by the letter P) are more modest types of hotel with fewer facilities. Both are graded with one to three stars. The letter R suffixed to a hotel or hostel sign means *residencia* and indicates that there is no restaurant.

Valencia's best hotels get booked up quickly for trade fairs and the Fallas festival in March. In general, prices are quoted per room and breakfast is rarely included. Value added tax (IVA) may or may not be included so it is best to confirm this. When checking in you will be asked to surrender your passport for a short period while the details are copied from it.

> I'd like a double/single room. **Quisiera una habitación doble/individual**
> with/without bath/shower double bed **con/sin baño/ducha cama de matrimonio**
> What's the rate per night? **¿Cuál es el precio por noche?**
> Is breakfast included? **¿Está incluído el desayuno?**

AIRPORTS

Valencia's international airport is at Manises (tel: 902 404 704 91 321 1000), 8.5km (5 miles) from the city centre. You can get to the centre by Aero-Bus (every 20 minutes 6am–10pm; €2.50). There are stops on Avenida del Cid (by the police station) and Calle Ángel Guimerá (junction with Calle Juan Llorens). Alternatively, you can take a slower line 150 bus (€1.45, concessions for families, journey takes about 40 min., operates Mon–Sat), metro lines 3 or 5 to the centre; line 5 goes all the way to the port via a tram link (see page 134). Taxis line up outside the arrivals hall and charge around €20 for the ride into the centre.

B

BEACHES

Valencia's warm climate means that the many long, sandy beaches accessible from the city can be enjoyed for several months of the year. They get busy during the holiday period of July and August (especially the latter), and at weekends in June and early September.

The **Playa de Las Arenas** and **Playa de la Malvarrosa** together comprise the city's main beach, which is easy to reach from the city centre by buses 95, 99, 32, 31, 1, 2 and 19, the tramway (line 4) or metro (lines 6, 8).

The two most popular beaches to the north of Valencia are **La Pobla de Farnals** and **Port Saplaya**, both within easy reach by car. To the south the principal beaches are **Playa de Pinedo** (6km/4 miles from Valencia) and **Playa del Saler** (12km/7.5 miles), which are reached by taking the motorway to the town of El Saler and then the coast road, CV-500. There is also a bus service there.

BICYCLE HIRE

Valencia is an ideal city for cycling around, being flat with a warm, dry climate, and an excellent network of cycle lanes. The local transport company (www.metrovalencia.com) provides information on 18 'Bicimetro' cycle routes that can be accessed using the metro. The city's public bike system is called Valenbisi (www.valenbisi.com) and offers a simple, efficient and comfortable way to move around. Otherwise, bicycles can be hired from the following:

Cyclobikes Valencia Turia gardens, next to the Gulliver Park, tel: 64 600 67 99, www.cyclotourbike.com; also hires two- and four-seater, pedal-powered cars.

Orange Bikes c/Guillem Sorolla 1, tel: 96 391 75 51, www.orangebikes.net.

Do You Bike Calle del Mar 14, tel: 96 315 55 51, www.doyoubike.com.
Valencia Guías Calle Turia 67; tel: 96 385 17 40, www.valenciaguias.com. Guided bicycle tours around the city.

BUDGETING FOR YOUR TRIP

Transport to Valencia. For Europeans, Valencia is a short and direct scheduled flight away from many major cities. Budget operators have made flying within Europe much more competitive; however, if you are travelling from beyond Europe the flight will be a considerably greater proportion of your overall budget.

Accommodation. Hotels in Valencia are quite expensive, but many offer special off-peak deals. A cheaper, though less convenient, option is to stay outside Valencia. It is always wise to book ahead.

Meals. Restaurant prices are not cheap, though with favourable exchange rates, even top-rated restaurants may be surprisingly affordable compared to many European capitals. The *menú del día*, a fixed-price midday meal, is an excellent bargain available in most restaurants, even fancy ones. Spanish wines are reasonably priced.

Local Transport. The sights in the city centre are mostly within walking distance of each other, making public transport use often unnecessary. Public transport in Valencia is inexpensive and even taxis are an affordable way to get around.

Museums. Many of Valencia's museums and galleries charge for admission. Note that many institutions are free on Sundays and closed on Mondays. See also Valencia Tourist Card.

Valencia Tourist Card. This card permits the holder to travel free on public transport (including the airport route) and gives discounts on entry to museums and other tourist sights, entertainment venues, shops and restaurants. It is available in one-, two- or three-day forms for €15, €20 and €25 respectively (there is also a 7-day card without transport for €10), from tourist information offices, bus stations, hotels, tobacconists, and on-line (with a 10 percent discount). For more details, tel: 90 070 18 18; or go to www.valenciatouristcard.com.

C

CAMPING

Valencia's climate makes camping quite easy for most of the year. There are three campsites to the south of the city, close to the sea and the Albufera nature reserve: **Camping Coll-Vert**, Playa de Pinedo, Carretera del Riu, 486, tel: 96 183 00 36, www.collvertcamping.com; **Camping Devesa Gardens**, Carretera del Saler, km 13, tel: 96 161 11 36, www.devesagardens.com; and **Camping Puzol**, Camí riu Turia 3, Playa de Puzol, tel: 96 142 15 27, www.campingpuzol.com.

CAR HIRE

You won't need a car to move around the city because the transport system is so good and, besides, finding a parking space is often tricky. But if you decide to make trips beyond the urban area you'll find your own transport will give you more flexibility.

The **Enterprise Rent a Car** (www.enterprise.com) has an office at Valencia airport (tel: 961 52 27 13), as do other major international car-hire companies, including **Avis** (tel: 902 110 195, www.avis.es); **Hertz** (tel: 96 152 37 91, www.hertz.es); and **Europcar** (tel: 902 50 30 10, www.europcar.es).

To hire a car you must be over 21 and have had your driving licence for at least a year – citizens of the EU can use their normal licences; other nationals need an international one.

> I'd like to hire a car tomorrow/for one day/a week **Quisiera alquilar un coche para mañana/por un día/una semana**
> Please include full insurance. **Haga el favor de incluir el seguro a todo riesgo.**
> unleaded petrol **gasolina sin plomo**
> Fill it up. **Lleno, por favor.**

CLIMATE

Valencia receives sunshine for most of the year, and has an average annual temperature of 17ºC (63ºF). The best seasons to visit are spring and autumn, although sometimes there is light rainfall in both. Summers can be hot and humid, but winters are mild, with a temperature which rarely falls below 10ºC (50ºF). The average monthly highs and lows are given below:

	J	F	M	A	M	J	J	A	S	O	N	D
ºC	13	14	16	18	21	25	28	28	25	21	16	13
	6	7	9	11	14	18	21	21	19	15	11	8
ºF	55	57	60	65	71	78	82	82	77	69	62	56
	43	45	48	52	57	65	69	69	66	58	51	46

CLOTHING

Valencians like to dress up. Although men are expected to wear jackets in elegant restaurants, smart-casual clothes will do most of the time. In the summer not many people go to restaurants wearing shorts unless the restaurant happens to be right on the beach. Women visiting churches should show respect by not wearing shorts or clothing that's too revealing. You will need a warm jacket from November to March, or a sweater and raincoat.

CRIME AND SAFETY

Valencia is one of the safest towns in Spain, but caution should be practised at all times as in any big city, especially in crowded metros or bars. Areas around the harbour or the Malvarrosa neighbourhood can be dangerous at night and it is advisable to avoid small, unlit streets and parks everywhere after dark.

Otherwise precautions are: never leave your bags unattended; don't carry too much money with you; wear your camera strapped to your body; and photocopy your personal documents and leave the originals in your hotel's safe, along with your valuables. Don't leave anything on display inside your car.

If you are the victim of a robbery, go to the nearest police station *(comisaría)* and make a report *(denuncia)*; you will need it for your insurance claim. For the local police, call 092.

> I want to report a theft. **Quiero denunciar un robo.**
> My ticket/wallet/passport has been stolen. **Me han robado mi billete/cartera/pasaporte.**

D

DRIVING

When driving in Spain you must be over 18 and carry with you the following documents: your passport, a valid driving licence, registration papers and a Green Card (international insurance certificate for non-EU countries) or a national insurance certificate (EU member states).

Road conditions. Outside of the morning and evening rush hours, Valencia's roads aren't too congested for a big city. However, there are big traffic jams on entry roads into the city on Sunday evenings and after holiday weekends.

Motorways. Valencia city and province are well served by main roads and motorways. The A7 motorway coming from the north (Catalonia) and going towards the south (Alicante) is a toll road *(autopista)*. The motorway that goes to the west (Madrid) is toll-free *(autovía)*.

Rules and regulations. You should display a nationality sticker on your car. Most fines for traffic offences are payable on the spot. Driving is on the right and overtaking (passing) is on the left. Give right of way to vehicles coming from the right (unless your road is marked as having priority). The use of front and rear seat belts is compulsory.

Speed limits in Spain for cars are 120km/h (75mph) on motorways, 100km/h (62mph) on broad main roads (two lanes each way), 90km/h (56mph) on other main roads, 50km/h (31mph), or as marked, in densely populated areas.

> driving licence **carnet de conducir**
> car registration papers **permiso de circulación**
> Can I park here? **¿Se puede aparcar aquí?**
> Are we on the right road for...?**¿Es ésta la carretera hacia...?**
> Where does this road lead? **¿Adónde va esta carretera?**
> Fill the tank please **Llénelo, por favor,**
> top grade **con super.**
> petrol **gasolina**
> unleaded petrol **gasolina sin plomo**
> diesel gasoléo
> Please check the oil/tyres/battery **Por favor, controle el aceite/los neumáticos/la batería.**
> I've broken down **Mi coche se ha estropeado.**
> There's been an accident **Ha habido un accidente.**

Always carry your driving licence and/or international driving permit with you. As the police can demand to see your passport at any time, it is also a good idea to carry a photocopy of its important pages.

Spanish law requires that your car should carry a reflective safety jacket in the event of a roadside emergency and a warning triangle. Seat belts are compulsory and children under the age of 12 or measuring less than 135cm in height can travel on the front seat if they are in a child restraint system adapted to their size and weight.

Breakdowns. Spanish garages are efficient and spare parts are readily available for most common makes of car. If you are an affiliated member of the RAC, you may call on the services of the Real Automóvil Club de España, tel: 900 112 222 (roadside assistance), which has its Valencia headquarters at Gran Vía Marqués de Turia 79, tel: 96 334 55 22.

Road signs. Some of the street names and signs are in Valencian. Most essential road signs, however, use the standard European pictographs. The translations below could be useful:

> **¡alto!** stop!
> **aparcamiento** parking
> **autopista (de peaje/peatge)** (toll) motorway (expressway)
> **ceda el paso** give way (yield)
> **curva peligrosa** dangerous bend
> **despacio** slow
> **desviación** diversion (detour)
> **estacionamiento prohibido** no parking
> **obras** roadworks
> **¡pare!** stop!
> **peatones** pedestrians
> **peligro** danger
> **salida** exit (from motorway)

E

ELECTRICITY

The standard is 220-volt. Sockets take round, two-pin plugs. Transformers and adapters can be bought in most hardware shops. Visitors from North America will need a transformer unless they have dual-voltage travel appliances.

EMBASSIES AND CONSULATES

All embassies are in the national capital, Madrid.

Australia: Paseo de la Castellana 259D, tel: 91 353 6600; www.spain.embassy.gov.au
Canada: Paseo de la Castellana 259D, tel: 91 382 8400; www.canadainternational.gc.ca
Ireland: Paseo de la Castellana 46-4, tel: 91 436 4093; www.dfa.ie/irish-embassy/Spain/
New Zealand: Pinar 7, 3rd floor, tel: 91 523 0226; www.nzembassy.com/spain
South Africa: Calle de Claudio Coello 91-6, tel: 91 436 3780; www.dirco.gov.za/madrid/en/
UK: Paseo de la Castellana 259D, tel: 91 714 6300; www.gov.uk/world/organisations/british-embassy-madrid
US: Calle de Serrano 75, tel: 91 587 2200; https://es.usembassy.gov/ US honorary consulate in Valencia; Doctor Romagosa 1 (2nd floor), tel: 96 351 69 73

EMERGENCIES

National Police *(policía nacional)*, in and outside Valencia: **091**
Local police *(policía local)*: **092**
Fire *(bomberos)*: **080**
Emergencies *(emergencias)*: **112**
Guardia civil (outside the city): **062**

> Fire! **¡Fuego!**
> Help! **¡Socorro!**
> Stop! **¡Deténgase!**
> Call the police/an ambulance **Llame a la policía/una ambulancia**
> Where is the nearest hospital? **¿Dónde está el hospital más próximo?**

GETTING THERE

By air. Extended in 2012, Valencia's airport (see page 114) receives direct scheduled flights from airports across Spain and Europe. Flights from the rest of the world go via Madrid and Barcelona. Spain's national carrier is Iberia (tel: 90 111 15 00, www.iberia.es). The low-cost carriers with flights to and from Valencia are Ryanair (www.ryanair.com), Monarch (www.monarch.es), and easyJet (www.easyjet.com).

By sea. Valencia port (www.valenciaport.com) has ferry lines to the Balearic Islands operated by Trasmediterránea Estación Marítima (tel: 90 245 46 45, www.trasmediterranea.es) and Balearia (tel: 902 160 180, www.balearia.com).

By rail. Valencia is linked by rail with the main Spanish cities and with European cities via Barcelona. There are daily trains to Madrid, Seville, Alicante, Barcelona, Port Bou (the French border), Zaragoza and Bilbao. Spain's train company, RENFE (tel: 912 320 320 in Spain, tel: 91 774 40 40 international, www.renfe.es), operates two stations in Valencia: **Estación del Norte** (the main one) and **Estación del Cabañal**, near the seafront. Terminal of the high-speed AVE (Joaquín Sorolla station) trains is located about 800 metres south of the Estación del Norte.

By car. The region's principal routes, the A7 motorway (toll) and the N340 (north) and N332 (south) run along the coast. The latter two tend to be congested with lorries and they pass through many small towns, making the motorway by far the best option if you can afford it.

A toll-free motorway, the A3, connects Valencia with Madrid. Other major roads are the A23 to Teruel and Zaragoza and the A35 (south) motorway to Xàtiva, becoming the A31 to Albacete.

By coach (long-distance bus). Valencia's coach/bus station, the Estación de Autobuses (Avenida Menéndez Pidal, tel: 96 346 62 66), is next door to the Nuevo Centro shopping centre on the north bank of the Turia riverbed. It has coach links with the main Valencian and

Spanish cities, and some European cities via Barcelona. From the coach station, you can take a local bus or the metro to get to the city centre.

GUIDES AND TOURS

Guided tours. There are guided tours of the historical centre of Valencia in English Mon–Sat from 10.30am to noon starting at the fountain in Plaza de la Virgen (2 hours 15 minutes; adults: €17; children 8–16: €8, under 8 go free; for details see www.visitvalencia.com), tailored tours of the city, including visits to the opera and wineries, are organised by Valencia Guías; tel: 963 851 740, www.valenciaguias.com.

Bus turistic. This tourist bus takes three interesting routes, two around the city (Route A: Historic Valencia, Route B: Maritime Valencia); the third one out to La Albufera. You can get on and off it at any stop, and recorded commentary is in English and other languages. Buses leave from the Plaza de la Reina (see details at www.visitvalencia.com). Tickets are valid 24 or 48 hours and cost €16–30 (adults); €9/11 (7-16 years) and can be bought on the bus or online as well as at tourist information offices.

> We'd like an English-speaking guide. **Queremos un guía que hable inglés.**
> I need an English interpreter. **Necesito un intérprete de inglés.**

H

HEALTH AND MEDICAL CARE

Residents of the European Union should carry with them the European Health Insurance Card or EHIC, available from post offices

HEALTH AND MEDICAL CARE

or online at www.ehic.org.uk, which entitles them to free medical treatment (with some exceptions) within the EU.

Be careful not to overdo the sunbathing in the first couple of days. Falling asleep on the beach is a common cause. Take the sun in short doses for at least the first few days, using a high-factor sunscreen; and drink plenty of bottled water *(agua mineral)* to avoid dehydration.

If you need a doctor in an emergency, call 112, or go to the **Hospital Universitario La Fe emergency unit** (Avinguda de Fernando Abril Martorell, no. 106; tel: 96 124 40 00; www.hospital-lafe.com) or the **Hospital Clínico Universitario** (Blasco Ibañez 17; tel: 96 197 35 00; http://clinicomalvarrosa.san.gva.es/hospital).

For non-emergencies, you may be able to solve the problem by visiting a *farmacia*, a chemist's shop, indicated by a green cross sign. Pharmacists are trained to give advice on treating common ailments and sometimes can prescribe without consulting a doctor. *Farmacias* are open during normal shopping hours. Out of hours, there is always one designated *farmacia de guardia* open in a neighbourhood: its address will be posted in the window of other *farmacias*.

Where's the nearest (all-night) chemist? **¿Dónde está la farmacia (de guardia) más cercana?**
I need a doctor/dentist. **Necesito un médico/dentista.**
It hurts here. **Me duele aquí.**
an ambulance/hospital **una ambulancia/un hospital**
sunburn **quemadura del sol**
sunstroke **insolación**
a fever **fiebre**
an upset stomach **dolor de estómago**
insect bite **una picadura de insecto**

LANGUAGE

Valencia has two official languages, Valencian (*valenciano*), which is a variant of Catalan, and Spanish, more properly called Castilian (*castellano*, that is, the language of Castile). Both are legally recognised by the Spanish constitution and are used daily. Many street names are in Valencian, and official papers are usually in both languages. Overleaf are some common phrases in both Valencian and Castilian.

> English **Valencian/Castilian**
> good morning/good day **bon dia/buenos días**
> good afternoon/good evening **bona tarda/buenas tardes**
> goodnight **bona nit/buenas noches**
> please **si us plau/por favor**
> thank you **gràcies/gracias**
> you're welcome **de res/de nada**
> goodbye **adéu/adiós**

LOST PROPERTY

If you lose an item of value, report the loss to the Municipal Police or the Guardia Civil. Ask for a copy of the police report, which you will need to make an insurance claim once you are home.

> I've lost my wallet/handbag/passport. **He perdido mi cartera/bolso/pasaporte.**

MAPS

The tourist information office gives out good maps of the city centre, but if you want to visit the outskirts you will probably have to buy a more detailed map in a bookshop. **Regolf** (Calle de la Mar 47, tel: 96 392 23 62; www.libreriaregolf.com) is a specialist map shop. If you are thinking of walking in the countryside, you may want to buy a 1:50,000 army map.

One manifestation of the upheavals that post-Franco Valencia has been undergoing is in the changing names of streets and squares, some of which have been confusingly re-baptised. The Plaza del Ayuntamiento, for example, was previously called the Plaza del Caudillo, after the rank Franco gave himself. Sometimes locals will refer to the old name of a street or square when giving directions. Here are a few *valenciano* street signs:

> English **Valencian/Castilian**
> avenue **avinguda/avenida**
> street **carrer/calle**
> church **església/iglesia**
> palace **palau/palacio**
> boulevard **passeig/paseo**
> square **plaça/plaza**
> a street plan of... **un plano de la ciudad de...**
> a road map of... **mapa de carreteras de...**

MEDIA

Major British and continental newspapers are on sale the same day as publication in newspaper kiosks in the city centre, as well as in the train station and the airport.

There are seven main Spanish TV channels, most dedicated largely to sport, foreign films and game shows. Better-equipped hotels receive non-Spanish satellite TV channels. Travellers with short-wave radios will be able to pick up the BBC World Service and the Voice of America.

> Have you got any English-language newspapers? **¿Tienen periódicos en inglés?**

MONEY

Currency. The monetary unit of Spain is the euro (€); with one hundred cents making 1 euro. Coins: cents 1, 2, 5, 10, 20 and 50, and euros 1 and 2. Banknotes: euros 5, 10, 20, 50, 100, 200 and 500.

Banking hours are usually Monday–Friday 8.30am–2.30pm. Only a few branches are open on Saturday mornings. Automatic Teller Machines (*cajeros automáticos*) are everywhere, and from them you can draw funds in euros against your bank account with a credit/debit card, although your bank may charge a handling fee.

Changing money. Many travel agencies display a *cambio* sign, meaning they will change foreign currency. Most hotels will also change money, albeit at a slightly less favourable rate than at the bank. Traveller's cheques always get a better rate than cash. Take your passport with you when changing money.

> Where's the nearest bank? **¿Dónde está el banco más cercano?**
> I want to change some pounds/dollars **Quiero cambiar libras/dólares**
> Do you accept traveller's cheques? **¿Acepta usted cheques deviaje?**
> Can I pay with this credit card? **¿Puedo pagar con esta tarjeta de crédito?**

Credit cards and traveller's cheques are accepted in most hotels, restaurants and big shops.

O

OPENING TIMES

Shops. Usual opening hours are Monday–Saturday 10am–8.30pm. The big department stores open all day 10am–9/10pm. Shops are closed on Sundays except on special occasions such as the run-up to Christmas.

Post offices. Generally open Monday–Friday 9am–2pm and Saturday 9am–1pm.

Banks. Usually open Monday–Friday 8.30am–2.30pm.

Government offices and most businesses. Open Monday–Friday 8.30am–2pm (government institutions) and 9am–8pm (business companies).

Restaurants. Mealtimes in Spain are later than in the rest of Europe. Breakfast is served between 7.30 and 10am. Lunch is 2–3.30pm, and dinner generally 9–10.30pm.

Museums. Generally, these are open Tuesday–Saturday 10am–8pm, some close for lunch, and most are closed Monday.

Entertainment venues. Most cinemas have several showings a day between 4pm and 11pm. Some theatres offer two performances a day at 6pm and 10pm. Pubs and musical venues are open between 9pm and 3am and discos 11.30pm–5am.

P

PHOTOGRAPHY

All popular types of discs, cards and batteries are widely available. Wherever possible, ask people for their permission before you take their picture. It is forbidden to take photographs of any military bases, military or naval port areas, police or military personnel.

POLICE

Valencia has two kinds of police force: the national police (policía nacional), dealing with serious crime, and the local police (policía local) in charge of public order. Spain has a third police force, the civil guard (Guardia Civíl), which operates in the countryside and patrols the main roads. In Valencia, dial **092** for the local police and **091** for the national police. The main local police station is located at Avenida del Cid 37, tel: 96 208 50 92.

> Where's the nearest police station? **¿Dónde está la comisaría más cercana?**

POST OFFICES

Spanish post offices have white and yellow signs saying 'Correos y Telégrafos'. You can send mail but not phone from them. They are usually open Monday–Friday 9am–2pm and Saturday 9am–1pm. If you just need stamps, get them from any tobacconist (estanco). Mailboxes (buzón de correos) are yellow.

Valencia's main post office is at Plaza del Ayuntamiento 24, tel: 96 351 27

> Where is the (nearest) post office? **¿Dónde está la oficina de correos (más cercana)?**
> Have you received any mail for...? **¿Ha recibido correo para...?**
> A stamp for this letter/postcard, please **Por favor, un sello para esta carta/tarjeta**
> express (special delivery) **urgente**
> airmail **via aérea**
> registered **certificado**

30. It is open Monday–Friday 8.30am–8.30pm and Saturday 9.30am–2pm.

PUBLIC HOLIDAYS
1 January Año Nuevo
6 January Epifanía (Día de Reyes)
22 January San Vicente Mártir
19 March San José (Las Fallas)
1 May Fiesta del Trabajo
15 August Asunción de Nuestra Señora (Virgen de agosto)
9 October Día de la Comunidad Valenciana
12 October Día de la Hispanidad
1 November Todos los Santos
6 December Día de la Constitución
8 December La Inmaculada Concepción
25 December Navidad
Movable dates:
Late March/April Viernes Santo
Late March/April Lunes de Pascua
Late March/April San Vicente Ferrer

R

RELIGION
The national religion of Spain is Roman Catholicism, and mass takes place in almost all the city's churches. Anglican services are held on Sunday mornings at the Iglesia de Jesucristo, Calle Dos de Abril 36, tel: 96 344 43 07, http://iglesiaanglicanavalencia.org.

For details of Muslim worship contact Centro Cultural Islámico de Valencia, Arquitecto Rodriguez 17, tel: 96 360 33 30, www.webcciv.org.

The Jewish community is served by the Javurá synagogue (Calle Uruguay 59, door 13, tel: 96 380 21 29, www.lajavura.org), which is affiliated to the United Synagogue of Conservative Judaism and the World Council of Conservative Synagogues.

TELEPHONES

Spain's country code is **34**. Valencia's provincial area code, **96**, must be dialled before all phone numbers, even for local calls.

You can make local, national and international calls from public phone booths *(cabinas)* in the streets, which operate with coins or cards. Instructions are given in several languages and some admit international credit cards. Phone cards *(tarjetas telefónicas)* can be purchased at tobacconists *(estancos)*, post offices or newsstands.

You can also make calls at public telephone centres called locutorios which are quieter than phone boxes and more convenient than fiddling with coins, as you pay over the counter when you have finished your call. Calls from a hotel room are usually more expensive than calls from phone boxes or *locutorios*. If you must phone from your hotel, ask in advance how much a three-minute call will cost. Reversed charge calls (collect) made to European Union countries can be dialled directly, otherwise they must be made through the operator.

To make an international call, dial **00** + country code + phone number, omitting the initial zero. The country code for the UK is **44**, for US and Canada **1**, for Australia **61** and for Ireland **353**.

Calls are cheaper after 10pm on weekdays, after 2pm on Saturday and all day on Sunday.

For national and international information dial **11888**. You can also find phone numbers at www.paginasamarillas.es and www.paginasblancas.es. For any other information on telephoning in Spain, see www.telefonica.es.

TIME ZONES

Spanish time coincides with that of most of Western Europe: Greenwich Mean Time plus one hour. In spring, clocks are put forward an hour, maintaining the one-hour difference.

New York	London	Spain	Sydney	Auckland
6am	11am	noon	8pm	10pm

TIPPING

A service charge is normally included in hotel and restaurant bills, and tipping is not obligatory, but it is the normal practice to leave a little small change if the service was satisfactory. If you want to tip a taxi driver, 5 percent will be enough. A common Spanish way of tipping in all circumstances is to round up the bill to the nearest euro or so.

TOILETS

There are not many public toilets in Valencia. Usually the most convenient option is to use those in a department store like El Corte Inglés, or in a bar or café – in the latter cases, it is polite to buy a drink.

In Spanish there are several words for toilets, the most common are *servicios*, *aseos* and *lavabos*.

TOURIST INFORMATION

The main tourist offices for the city are:

Calle de la Paz 48, tel: 96 398 64 22. Open Monday–Sat 9am– 6.50pm, Saturday 10am–1.30pm. For information about the city and the whole Valencian region.

Plaza del Ayuntamiento 1, tel: 96 352 49 08. Open Mon–Sat 9am–6.50pm, Sun 10am–1.50pm.

Estación del Norte (the main railway station), tel: 96 380 36 23.

Tourist Info-Diputación, Poeta Querol (near the Teatro Principal), tel: 96 351 49 07 for information about Valencia province.

Airport (arrivals hall), tel: 96 153 02 29.

Tourist-info Beach, Paseo de Neptuno 2 (in front of Hotel Neptuno), Tue and Sun10am–1.50pm, Wed, Fri and Sat 10am–1.50pm and 2.50–4.50pm (open in summer only).

TRANSPORT

Valencia has a fast and reliable public transport network reaching almost everywhere a visitor would want to go. Fares are quite reasonable, too.

By bus. Valencia's fleet of red buses is operated by EMT (Empresa Municipal de Transportes de Valencia), tel: 96 346 62 66, www.emtvalencia.es. There are 47 regular routes during the day and 12 night ones. At most bus stops there are maps of the city with all the routes marked. A single-trip bus ticket costs €1.50, but if you are going to be using buses a lot, buy a *bonobus* (€8.50), valid for 10 trips, from a tobacconist's *(estanco)*.

By metro and tramway. Valencia's metro network is run by FGV (Ferrocarriles Generalitat Valenciana; www.fgv.es). Modern, clean and reliable, it is organised into nine lines (Nos 1–9) that link the city centre with nearby towns:

Línea 1: Llíria (northwest) and Bétera (north) to Torrent (southwest) and Villanueva de Castellón (near Xàtiva, 40km/25 miles) to the southwest.

Línea 2: runs from Llíria (northwest) to Torrent Avinguda (south) through the city centre.

Línea 3: the most frequently used line goes from Rafelbunyol (north) to the Airport (west).

Línea 4: Ll. Larga-Terramelar, Feria Valencia (north) and Mas del Rosari (north) to Doctor Lluch (east). This line is a modern tramway serving the city's beaches – depart from Pont de Fusta station.

Línea 5: Marítim Serrería (east) to the Airport (west) and Torrent (southwest).

Línea 6: A tramway linking Tossal del Rei (Rascanya; north) with the seaside and Marítim Serrería (Poblados Marítimos) in the east.

Línea 7: **Connects** Torrent (southwest) and Marítim Serrería (east)

Línea 8: A tram line connecting Marítim Serrería (east) with the port (Marina Real Juan Carlos I).

Línea 9: Links Riba-roja de Turia (west) with Alboraya Peris Aragó (northeast).

> When is the next bus/train for...? **¿A qué hora sale el próximo autobús/tren para...?**
> I want a ticket to... **Quiero un billete para...**
> What's the fare to...? **¿Cuánto es la tarifa a ...?**
> single (one-way) **ida**
> return (round-trip) **ida y vuelta**
> Where can I get a taxi? **¿Dónde puedo coger un taxi?**

The main interchanges are Empalme, Benimaclet, Colón, Rosas, Marítim Serrería, and Angel Guimera. Fares are from €1.50 for a single ticket and from €7.20 (one zone) for a *bonometro*, a ticket valid for 10 trips. For more information, see www.metrovalencia.com.

By taxi. Taxis (always white cars) are everywhere and are not too expensive. You can hail one in the street or go to a taxi rank. It may be hard to find one during the peak periods of 8–9pm and 1–2pm. A green light or a *libre* sign shows that a taxi is available for hire. There are two kinds of tariff: one for daytime (6am–10pm) trips within the urban area; the other for night time and journeys outside the city limits.

Taxi companies include the following: Onda-Taxi, tel: 96 347 52 52; Radio-Taxi, tel: 96 370 33 33; Valencia Taxi, tel: 96 374 02 02; Taxi Star, tel: 639 61 66 66; and Tele-Taxi, tel: 96 357 13 13.

V

VISAS AND ENTRY REQUIREMENTS

Most visitors, including citizens of all EU countries, the US, Canada, Australia and New Zealand, require only a valid passport – not a visa or a health certificate – to enter Spain.

Visitors from South Africa should apply in advance for a Schengen visa, and passports should be valid for at least three months beyond the expiry date of your visa. If you expect to remain for longer than 90 days, a Spanish consulate or tourist office can advise you of the necessary steps to take.

W

WEBSITES AND INTERNET ACCESS

Most hotels in Valencia have internet connections and there are many areas of the city covered by WiFi (for details see https://wifispc.com/spain/galicia/valencia.html).

www.visitvalencia.com The official city's tourist website, in various languages.

www.valencia.es The city hall's site.

www.valencia-on-line.com Another useful general site (also a booking agency).

www.comunitatvalenciana.com Information on the region, including the Costa Blanca and Costa del Azahar.

www.valencia-cityguide.com A comprehensive city guide and information site on Valencia.

www.spain.info Spain's national tourism website.

Y

YOUTH HOSTELS

Valencia has several youth hostels including:

Albergue Juvenil Center Valencia, Calle Samaniego 18, tel: 96 391 49 15. Offers 2, 4, 6 and 8 bed accommodation.

Red Nest Hostel, Calle Paz 36, tel: 96 342 71 68

Purple Nest Hostel, Plaza de Tetuán 5, tel: 96 353 25 61

Albergue Juvenil Colegio Mayor Galileo Galilei, Av. de los Naranjos, tel: 96 335 20 00.

For more information, contact Red Española de Albergues Juveniles, Calle Marqués de Riscal 16, 28010 Madrid; tel: 91 308 46 75, www.reaj.com.

RECOMMENDED HOTELS

Spanish hotels are graded one to five stars depending upon facilities. Some establishments are classified as *hostales* (with one to three stars) and others *pensiones* – these are not necessarily less welcoming or less comfortable than a hotel of higher rank. The suffix *residencia* to a hotel or *hostal* means that there is no dining room, although breakfasts may still be served.

In a class of their own are *paradores*, state-run hotels which either occupy historic buildings or are purpose-built in privileged locations. Either way, a *parador* offers a reliable level of comfort and its restaurant specialises in the cuisine of the region. El Saler is the *parador* closest to Valencia; the next closest are Jávea on the Costa Blanca and Benicarló on the Costa del Azahar.

The following guide indicates prices for a double room in high season. These should be used as an approximation only as prices can vary widely and even expensive hotels can sometimes offer competitive deals for weekend stays.

€€€€ over 200 euros
€€€ 120–200 euros
€€ 80–120 euros
€ below 80 euros

CITY CENTRE

Ad Hoc Monumental €€€ *Calle Boix 4, tel: 96 391 91 40, www.adhochoteles.com*. A charming little three-star hotel occupying a sensitively restored late 19th-century mansion on the edge of the old town near the river (between the Torres de Serranos and the Gobierno Civil). It has great character with its patio garden, exposed brickwork and beams, high ceilings and eclectic mixture of antique and modern furniture. Very close to the riverbed and the Museo de Bellas Artes (Museum of Fine Arts). Car, bicycle and Segway rental service. 28 rooms.

RECOMMENDED HOTELS

Antigua Morellana € *Calle En Bou 2, tel: 96 391 57 73*, www.hostalam.com. A small family-run hotel in an 18th-century building in a little street between La Lonja and Plaza de la Reina. The staff are friendly and some of the rooms have been newly refurbished. No dining room but there are restaurants not far away. Good value. 18 rooms.

Ayre Hotel Astoria Palace €€€–€€€€ *Plaza de Rodrigo Botet 5, tel: 96 398 10 00*, www.ayrehoteles.com. Located on a small square in the city centre, close to the Plaza del Ayuntamiento, the Astoria Palace is a big, luxurious and impeccably renovated hotel of long standing. It has a range of English-style, comfortable rooms as well as business and fitness centres, a restaurant and a bar. 217 rooms.

Chill Art Hotel Jardín Botánico €€–€€€ *Dr Peset Cervera 6, tel: 96 315 40 12*, http://jardinbotanicoboutique.com. This small hotel is, as its name suggests, close to the botanic gardens, a little way from the city centre proper. There is a bar and a café. 16 rooms.

Home Hostel € *Calle La Lonja 4, tel: 96 391 62 29*, www.homehostelsvalencia.com. A cheap and sociable guesthouse aimed at budget travellers – one step up from a youth hostel – and conveniently located in one of the old streets south of Calle Caballeros. The same organisation has another youth hostel for backpackers on Calle Vicente Iborra. Both establishments have a guest kitchen, internet access and helpful multilingual staff, and are open 24 hours a day. 10 rooms.

Hospes Palau de la Mar €€€ *Calle Navarro Reverter 14, tel: 900 925 500*, www.hospes.es. Completely renovated and featuring a contemporary, minimalist décor, this boutique hotel is sited within two 19th-century mansions on a busy street between the old town and the river. As well as a high-season rate, it has an extra-high season rate for important trade fairs and sporting fixtures. The restaurant serves a variety of the finest Valencian cuisine. 66 rooms.

Hostal Venecia €–€€ *Plaza del Ayuntamiento 3, tel: 96 352 42 67*, www.hotelvenecia.com. At the top (narrow) end of Plaza del Ayuntamiento with some rooms overlooking the square. The train station is just a three-minute walk away. The refurbished rooms are relatively plain with minimal decor, but clean and comfortable with a small bathroom. Internet access is available and there is an individual safe in each room. Rooms have been adapted for disabled guests. 66 rooms.

Hotel Casual de las Artes €€€ *Avenida del Puerto 39, tel: 96 362 54 32.* Conveniently located a short way up the street towards the port from the Palau de la Música is this four-star hotel in a building from the early 20th century. It has a heated indoor pool and sauna. Some of the rooms are in the attic. 62 rooms. Breakfast included.

Melia Valencia €€€ *Avenida Cortes Valencianas 52, tel: 96 303 00 00,* www.melia-valencia.com. A sumptuous four-star hotel with spacious modern rooms looking over the gardens in the bed of the River Turia. A little far from the city centre, it is well located for a visit to the City of Arts and Sciences. Excellent spa, pool, gym and convention centre. 303 rooms.

One Shot Palacio Reina Victoria €€€ *Barcas 4–6, tel: 963 513 984,* www.hotelonesshotpalacioreinavictoria04.com/. A few minutes' walk from the railway station, and overlooking Plaza del País Valenciano, this is Valencia's grandest hotel. The art-nouveau establishment, which opened in 1913, still has an old-fashioned feel, although it has been modernised. Over the years, the roll-call of distinguished guests has included Picasso, Dalí, García Lorca and Miró, as well as King Alfonso XIII and Queen Victoria. The Little Queen restaurant serves regional dishes. 85 rooms.

SH Inglés €€€ *Marqués de Dos Aguas 6, tel: 96 351 64 26,* www.inglesboutique.com. A modern, three-star chain hotel behind the 19th-century façade of the former mansion of the Cardona family. Centrally located next to the Palacio del Marqués de Dos Aguas (Ceramics Museum). Some rooms have large balconies. 63 rooms.

SEAFRONT

Las Arenas €€€ *Eugenia Vines 22–24, tel: 96 312 06 00,* www.hotelvalencialasarenas.com. A five-star spa resort on the Paseo Marítimo incorporating elements of a 1930s spa, including the swimming pool. It has large lounges and a garage, restaurants and a café-bar. 253 rooms.

Neptuno €€€ *Paseo Neptuno 2, tel: 96 356 77 77, www.hotelneptuno valencia.com*. A modern luxury hotel on the beach next to a line of restaurants specialising in paella. Rooms have hydromassage baths, plasma TV screens and internet access. About 10 rooms face the sea; book early to get one. Restaurant, gym, jacuzzi and sauna. 50 rooms.

OUTSKIRTS

Ad Hoc Parque Golf €€ *Urbinazación Torre en Conill 6-8, Bétera (17km/ 11.5 miles from Valencia), tel: 96 169 83 93, www.adhochoteles.com*. A four-star rural hotel belonging to the owners of the city centre Ad Hoc Monumental. Located opposite the Escorpión Golf Club Garden it has a garden terrace, a swimming pool and a first-class restaurant (La Sal) 41 rooms.

Hotel Albufera € *Plaza Alqueria de La Culla, Albufera, tel: 96 318 65 56, www.hotelalbufera.com*. A non-nonsense proposal for those willing to explore nearby Albufera beaches. Well-communicated with the city centre, not far from the City of Arts, it offers modern rooms, gym, swimming pool and free parking. Buffet breakfast included. A commercial centre is close-by. 98 rooms.

Hotel La Mozaira €€€ *Camí del Machistre 50, Alboraya, tel: 961 85 09 24, www.lamozaira.com*. A renovated 17th-century whitewashed *alquería*, not far from the city and only a 10-minute walk from the sea. It stands in the huerta and is surrounded by tigernut fields, the ingredient of Valencia's famous summer drink, *horchata*. The restaurant serves organic vegetables from the hotel's own garden.

Hotel Olympia €-€€ *C/ Maestro Serrano 3-5, Alboraya (north from city centre), tel: 96 303 33 92, www.olympiahotelvalencia.com*. This modern hotel with adjacent spa offers spacious air-conditioned rooms at accessible prices. Buffet meals are abundant and varied. Metro station is within walking distance which makes it a good base for exploring the city. Indoor swimming pool and conference centre also available. 167 rooms.

Parador de El Saler €€€ *Avenida de los Pinares 151 (18km/11 miles from the city centre by motorway; 17km/10½ miles from the airport), tel: 96 161 11 86*, www.parador.es. Part of the state-run chain of plush hotels, this is an elegant refuge from the city next to a nature reserve and the sea, and surrounded by an internationally known golf course. The restaurant serves paella and other typical Valencian dishes. 65 rooms. Next to the *parador* there is a professional golf course said to have one of the best layouts in the world. It was designed by the internationally recognised "architect of Spanish golf", Javier Arana. Bookings can be made directly with the *parador* or via Paradores de Turismo de España, Requena 3, 28013 Madrid, tel: 90 254 79 79 or the *paradores*' agent in the UK, Keytel International, The Foundry, 156 Blackfriars Rd, London SE1 8EN, tel: 0800 160 1013, www.keytel.co.uk.

Tryp Oceanic €€€ *C/ Pintor Maella 35, tel: 96 335 03 00*, www.tryphotels.com. This modern hotel with 197 rooms is conveniently situated close to the City of Arts and Sciences, harbour and large commercial centre. Gym is available to guests 24 hours a day and has magnificent views over the city. There is also a swimming pool and Finnish sauna. Staff are friendly and efficient.

DENIA

Hotel El Raset €€ *Calle Bellavista 1, tel: 96 578 65 64*, www.hotelelraset.com. Next to the harbour of Denia, this small hotel makes an excellent base from which to explore the Costa Blanca and El Montgó National Park. It is superbly situated just 2 minutes from the town centre and just a minute walk from the beach. This traditional building offers 20 modern rooms.

GANDIA

RH Bayren Hotel&Spa €€€ *Paseo de Neptuno 62, Playa Gandia, tel: 965 85 39 39*, www.hotelesrh.com. A modern complex opposite the spectacular Playa Gandia with several pools (including one indoors), spa, sauna, its own beach bar and a restaurant. Some suites offer splendid views over the sea from large balconies.

XATIVA

Casa Aldomar € *Calle Bosh 11, tel: 96 227 65 63*, www.casa-aldomar.com. A beautiful 18th century house on the pedestrianised street in the heart of the old quarter. Carefully renovated it offers four air-conditioned rooms that combine modern design with traditional rural materials. Breakfast and free internet.

Mont Sant €€€ *Subida al Castillo, tel: 96 227 50 81*, http://mont-sant.com. A country house built on the ruins of a monastery at the foot of Xàtiva's castle, of which it has good views. It is surrounded by beautiful landscaped gardens. The rooms on the top floor of the main building have excellent views of Xàtiva. 17 rooms.

PENISCOLA

Hotel Agora Spa & Resort €€–€€€ *Calle Huerto 8, tel: 902 88 63 86* www.agorahoteles.com. A spacious and ultramodern hotel in the La Cantera area of Peñíscola, only 50 metres from the sea and not far from the historic quarter. Bedrooms are spacious with plenty of natural light, and well insulated. There are several swimming pools and a spa.

Parador de Benicarlo €€€ *Avenida Papa Luna 5, tel: 96 447 01 00*, www.parador.es. A parador beside the sea with a large garden and a swimming pool. It's located about 8km (5 miles) along the coast from Peñíscola. 106 rooms.

DICTIONARY

ENGLISH–SPANISH

adj adjective **adv** adverb **BE** British English **n** noun **prep** preposition **v** verb

A

abbey la abadía
accept v aceptar
access el acceso
accident el accidente
accommodation el alojamiento
account la cuenta
acupuncture la acupuntura
adapter el adaptador
address la dirección
admission la entrada
after después; ~**noon** la tarde; ~**shave** el bálsamo para después del afeitado
age la edad
agency la agencia
AIDS el sida
air el aire; ~ **conditioning** el aire acondicionado; ~ **pump** el aire; ~**line** la compañía aérea; ~**mail** el correo aéreo; ~**plane** el avión; ~**port** el aeropuerto
aisle el pasillo; ~ **seat** el asiento de pasillo
allergic alérgico; ~ **reaction** la reacción alérgica
allow v permitir

alone solo
alter v **(clothing)** hacer un arreglo
alternate route el otro camino
aluminum foil el papel de aluminio
amazing increíble
ambulance la ambulancia
American estadounidense
amusement park el parque de atracciones
anemic anémico
anesthesia la anestesia
animal el animal
ankle el tobillo
antibiotic el antibiótico
antiques store la tienda de -antigüedades
antiseptic cream la crema antiséptica
anything algo
apartment el apartamento
appendix (body part) el apéndice
appetizer el aperitivo
appointment la cita
arcade el salón de juegos recreativos
area code el prefijo
arm el brazo

aromatherapy la aromaterapia
around (the corner) doblando (la esquina)
arrivals (airport) las llegadas
arrive v llegar
artery la arteria
arthritis la artritis
arts las letras
Asian asiático
aspirin la aspirina
asthmatic asmático
ATM el cajero automático
attack el asalto
attend v asistir
attraction (place) el sitio de interés
attractive guapo
Australia Australia
Australian australiano
automatic automático; ~ **car** coche automático
available disponible

B

baby el bebé; ~ **bottle** el biberón; ~ **wipe** la toallita; ~**sitter** el/la canguro
back la espalda; ~**ache** el dolor de espalda; ~**pack** la mochila

bag la maleta
baggage el equipaje; ~ **claim** la recogida de equipajes; ~ **ticket** el talón de equipaje
bakery la panadería
ballet el ballet
bandage la tirita
bank el banco
bar el bar
barbecue la barbacoa
barber la peluquería de caballeros
baseball el béisbol
basket (grocery store) la cesta
basketball el baloncesto
bathroom el baño
battery (car) la batería
battery la pila
battleground el campo de batalla
be v ser, estar
beach la playa
beautiful precioso
bed la cama; ~ **and breakfast** la pensión
begin v empezar
before antes de
beginner principiante
behind detrás de
beige beis
belt el cinturón

143

DICTIONARY

berth la litera
best el/la mejor
better mejor
bicycle la bicicleta
big grande
bigger más grande
bike route el sendero para bicicletas
bikini el biquini; **~ wax** la depilación de las ingles
bill v **(charge)** cobrar; **~** n **(money)** el billete; **~ (of sale)** el recibo
bird el pájaro
birthday el cumpleaños
black negro
bladder la vejiga
bland soso
blanket la manta
bleed v sangrar
blood la sangre; **~ pressure** la tensión arterial
blouse la blusa
blue azul
board v embarcar
boarding pass la tarjeta de embarque
boat el barco
bone el hueso
book el libro; **~store** la librería
boots las botas
boring aburrido
botanical garden el jardín botánico
bother v molestar
bottle la botella; **~ opener** el abrebotellas
bowl el cuenco
box la caja

boxing match la pelea de boxeo
boy el niño; **~friend** el novio
bra el sujetador
bracelet la pulsera
brakes (car) los frenos
break v romper
break-in (burglary) el allanamiento de morada
breakdown la avería
breakfast el desayuno
breast el seno; **~feed** dar el pecho
breathe v respirar
bridge el puente
briefs (clothing) los calzoncillos
bring v traer
British británico
broken roto
brooch el broche
broom la escoba
brother el hermano
brown marrón
bug el insecto
building el edificio
burn v **(CD)** grabar
bus el autobús; **~ station** la estación de autobuses; **~ stop** la parada de autobús; **~ ticket** el billete de autobús; **~ tour** el recorrido en autobús
business los negocios; **~ card** la tarjeta de negocios; **~ center** el centro de negocios; **~ class** la clase preferente; **~ hours** el horario de atención al público

butcher el carnicero
buttocks las nalgas
buy v comprar
bye adiós

C

cabaret el cabaré
cabin (house) la cabaña; **~ (ship)** el camarote
cable car el teleférico
cafe la cafetería
call v llamar; **~** n la llamada
calories las calorías
camera la cámara; **digital ~** la cámara digital; **~ case** la funda para la cámara; **~ store** la tienda de fotografía
camp v acampar; **~ stove** el hornillo; **~site** el cámping
can opener el abrelatas
Canada Canadá
Canadian canadiense
cancel v cancelar
candy el caramelo
canned goods las conservas
canyon el cañón
car el coche; **~ hire [BE]** el alquiler de coches; **~ park [BE]** el aparcamiento; **~ rental** el alquiler de coches; **~ seat** el asiento de niño
carafe la garrafa
card la tarjeta; **ATM ~** la tarjeta de cajero automático; **credit ~** la tarjeta de crédito; **debit ~** la tarjeta de débito; **phone ~** la tarjeta telefónica
carry-on (piece of hand luggage) el equipaje de mano
cart (grocery store) el carrito; **~ (luggage)** el carrito para el equipaje
carton el cartón; **~ of cigarettes** el cartón de tabaco
case (amount) la caja
cash v cobrar; **~** n el efectivo; **~ advance** sacar dinero de la tarjeta
cashier el cajero
casino el casino
castle el castillo
cathedral la catedral
cave la cueva
CD el CD
cell phone el teléfono móvil
Celsius el grado centígrado
centimeter el centímetro
certificate el certificado
chair la silla; **~ lift** la telesilla
change v **(buses)** cambiar; **~** n **(money)** el cambio
charcoal el carbón
charge v **(credit card)** cobrar; **~** n **(cost)** el precio
cheap barato
cheaper más barato

DICTIONARY

check v **(on something)** revisar; ~ v **(luggage)** facturar; ~ n **(payment)** el cheque; ~~**in (airport)** la facturación; ~~**in (hotel)** el registro; ~**ing account** la cuenta corriente; ~~**out (hotel)** la salida
Cheers! ¡Salud!
chemical toilet el váter químico
chemist [BE] la farmacia
cheque [BE] el cheque
chest (body part) el pecho; ~ **pain** el dolor de pecho
chewing gum el chicle
child el niño; ~ **seat** la silla para niños
children's menu el menú para niños
children's portion la ración para niños
Chinese chino
chopsticks los palillos chinos
church la iglesia
cigar el puro
cigarette el cigarrillo
class la clase; **business** ~ la clase preferente; **economy** ~ la clase económica; **first** ~ la primera clase
classical music la música clásica
clean v limpiar; ~ adj limpio; ~**ing product** el producto de limpieza; ~**ing supplies** los productos de limpieza
clear v **(on an ATM)** borrar
cliff el acantilado
cling film [BE] el film transparente
close v **(a shop)** cerrar
closed cerrado
clothing la ropa; ~ **store** la tienda de ropa
club la discoteca
coat el abrigo
coffee shop la cafetería
coin la moneda
colander el escurridor
cold n **(sickness)** el catarro; ~ adj **(temperature)** frío
colleague el compañero de trabajo
cologne la colonia
color el color
comb el peine
come v venir
complaint la queja
computer el ordenador
concert el concierto; ~ **hall** la sala de conciertos
condition (medical) el estado de salud
conditioner el suavizante
condom el preservativo
conference la conferencia
confirm v confirmar
congestion la congestión
connect v **(internet)** conectarse
connection (internet) la conexión; ~ **(flight)** la conexión de vuelo
constipated estreñido
consulate el consulado
consultant el consultor
contact v ponerse en contacto con
contact lens la lentilla de contacto; ~ **solution** el líquido de lentillas de contacto
contagious contagioso
convention hall el salón de congresos
conveyor belt la cinta transportadora
cook v cocinar
cooking gas el gas butano
cool (temperature) frío
copper el cobre
corkscrew el sacacorchos
cost v costar
cot el catre
cotton el algodón
cough v toser; ~ n la tos
country code el código de país
cover charge la entrada
crash v **(car)** estrellarse
cream (ointment) la pomada
credit card la tarjeta de crédito
crew neck el cuello redondo
crib la cuna
crystal el cristal
cup la taza
currency la moneda; ~ **exchange** el cambio de divisas; ~ **exchange office** la casa de cambio
current account [BE] la cuenta corriente
customs las aduanas
cut v **(hair)** cortar; ~ n **(injury)** el corte
cute mono
cycling el ciclismo

D

damage v causar daño
damaged ha sufrido daños
dance v bailar; ~ **club** la discoteca
dangerous peligroso
dark oscuro
date (calendar) la fecha
day el día
deaf sordo
debit card la tarjeta de débito
deck chair la tumbona
declare v declarar
decline v **(credit card)** rechazar
deeply hondo
degrees (temperature) los grados
delay v retrasarse
delete v **(computer)** borrar
delicatessen la charcutería
delicious delicioso
denim tela vaquero
dentist el dentista
denture la dentadura
deodorant el desodorante

department store los grandes almacenes
departures (airport) las salidas
deposit v depositar; ~ n **(bank)** el depósito bancario; ~ v **(reserve a room)** la fianza
desert el desierto
dessert el postre
detergent el detergente
develop v **(film)** revelar
diabetic diabético
dial v marcar
diamond el diamante
diaper el pañal
diarrhea la diarrea
diesel el diesel
difficult difícil
digital digital; ~ **camera** la cámara digital; ~ **photos** las fotos digitales; ~ **prints** las fotos digitales
dining room el comedor
dinner la cena
direction la dirección
dirty sucio
disabled discapacitado; ~ **accessible [BE]** el acceso para discapacitados
discharge (bodily fluid) la secreción
disconnect (computer) desconectar
discount el descuento
dish (kitchen) el plato; **~washer** el lavavajillas; **~washing liquid** el líquido lavavajillas
display v mostrar; ~ **case** la vitrina
disposable desechable; ~ **razor** la cuchilla desechable
dive v bucear
diving equipment el equipo de buceo
divorce v divorciar
dizzy mareado
doctor el médico
doll la muñeca
dollar (U.S.) el dólar
domestic nacional; ~ **flight** el vuelo nacional
door la puerta
dormitory el dormitorio
double bed la cama de matrimonio
downtown el centro
dozen la docena
drag lift el telesquí
dress (piece of clothing) el vestido; ~ **code** las normas de vestuario
drink v beber; ~ n la bebida; ~ **menu** la carta de bebidas; **~ing water** el agua potable
drive v conducir
driver's license number el número de permiso de conducir
drop (medicine) la gota
drowsiness la somnolencia
dry cleaner la tintorería
dubbed doblada
during durante
duty (tax) el impuesto; **~-free** libre de impuestos
DVD el DVD

E

ear la oreja; **~ache** el dolor de oído
earlier más temprano
early temprano
earrings los pendientes
east el este
easy fácil
eat v comer
economy class la clase económica
elbow el codo
electric outlet el enchufe eléctrico
elevator el ascensor
e-mail v enviar un correo electrónico; ~ n el correo electrónico; ~ **address** la dirección de correo electrónico
emergency la emergencia; ~ **exit** la salida de urgencia
empty v vaciar
enamel (jewelry) el esmalte
end v terminar
English el inglés
engrave v grabar
enjoy v disfrutar
enter v entrar
entertainment el entretenimiento
entrance la entrada
envelope el sobre
equipment el equipo
escalators las escaleras mecánicas
e-ticket el billete electrónico
EU resident el/la residente de la UE
euro el euro
evening la noche
excess el exceso
exchange v **(money)** cambiar; ~ v **(goods)** devolver; ~ n **(place)** la casa de cambio; ~ **rate** el tipo de cambio
excursion la excursión
excuse v **(to get past)** pedir perdón; ~ v **(to get attention)** disculparse
exhausted agotado
exit v salir; ~ n la salida
expensive caro
expert (skill level) experto
exposure (film) la foto
express rápido; ~ **bus** el autobús rápido; ~ **train** el tren rápido
extension (phone) la extensión
extra adicional; ~ **large** equis ele (XL)
extract v **(tooth)** extraer
eye el ojo
eyebrow wax la depilación de cejas

F

face la cara
facial la limpieza de cutis

DICTIONARY 147

family la familia
fan (appliance) el ventilador; **~ (souvenir)** el abanico
far lejos; **~-sighted** hipermétrope
farm la granja
fast rápido; **~ food** la comida rápida
faster más rápido
fat free sin grasa
father el padre
fax v enviar un fax; **~** n el fax; **~ number** el número de fax
fee la tasa
feed v alimentar
ferry el ferry
fever la fiebre
field (sports) el campo
fill v llenar ; **~ out** v **(form)** rellenar
filling (tooth) el empaste
film (camera) el carrete
fine (fee for breaking law) la multa
finger el dedo; **~nail** la uña del dedo
fire fuego; **~ department** los bomberos; **~ door** la puerta de incendios
first primero ; **~ class** la primera clase
fit (clothing) quedar bien
fitting room el probador
fix v **(repair)** reparar
flashlight la linterna
flight el vuelo

floor el suelo
flower la flor
folk music la música folk
food la comida
foot el pie
football [BE] el fútbol
for para/por
forecast el pronóstico
forest el bosque
fork el tenedor
form el formulario
formula (baby) la fórmula infantil
fort el fuerte
fountain la fuente
free gratuito
freezer el congelador
fresh fresco
friend el amigo
frying pan la sartén
full completo; **~-service** el servicio completo; **~-time** el tiempo completo

G

game el partido
garage (parking) el garaje; **~ (repair)** el taller
garbage bag la bolsa de basura
gas la gasolina; **~ station** la gasolinera
gate (airport) la puerta
gay gay; **~ bar** el bar gay; **~ club** la discoteca gay
gel (hair) la gomina
get to v ir a
get off v **(a train/bus/subway)** bajarse
gift el regalo; **~ shop** la tienda

de regalos
girl la niña; **~friend** la novia
give v dar
glass (drinking) el vaso; **~ (material)** el vidrio
glasses las gafas
go v **(somewhere)** ir a
gold el oro
golf golf; **~ course** el campo de golf; **~ tournament** el torneo de golf
good n el producto; **~** adj bueno; **~ afternoon** buenas tardes; **~ evening** buenas noches; **~ morning** buenos días; **~bye** adiós
gram el gramo
grandchild el nieto
grandparent el abuelo
gray gris
green verde
grocery store el supermercado
ground la tierra; **~ floor** la planta baja; **~cloth** la tela impermeable
group el grupo
guide la guía; **~ book** la guía; **~ dog** el perro guía
gym el gimnasio
gynecologist el ginecólogo

H

hair el pelo; **~ dryer** el secador de pelo; **~ salon** la peluquería; **~brush** el

cepillo de pelo; **~cut** el corte de pelo; **~spray** la laca; **~style** el peinado; **~stylist** el estilista
half medio; **~ hour** la media hora; **~-kilo** el medio kilo
hammer el martillo
hand la mano; **~ luggage [BE]** el equipaje de mano; **~bag [BE]** el bolso
handicapped discapacitado; **~-accessible** el acceso para discapacitados
hangover la resaca
happy feliz
hat el sombrero
have v tener
head (body part) la cabeza; **~ache** el dolor de cabeza; **~phones** los cascos
health la salud; **~ food store** la tienda de alimentos naturales
heart el corazón; **~ condition** padecer del corazón
heat v calentar; **~** n el calor
heater [heating BE] la calefacción
hello hola
helmet el casco
help v ayudar; **~** n la ayuda
here aquí
hi hola
high alto; **~chair** la trona; **~way** la autopista

hiking boots las botas de montaña
hill la colina
hire v [BE] alquilar; **~ car** [BE] el coche de alquiler
hitchhike v hacer autostop
hockey el hockey
holiday [BE] las vacaciones
horse track el hipódromo
hospital el hospital
hostel el albergue
hot (temperature) caliente; **~ (spicy)** picante; **~ spring** el agua termale; **~ water** el agua caliente
hotel el hotel
hour la hora
house la casa; **~hold goods** los artículos para el hogar; **~keeping services** el servicio de limpieza de habitaciones
how (question) cómo; **~ much (question)** cuánto cuesta
hug v abrazar
hungry hambriento
hurt v **(have pain)** tener dolor
husband el marido

I

ibuprofen el ibuprofeno
ice el hielo; **~ hockey** el hockey sobre hielo

icy adj helado
identification el documento de identidad
ill v **(to feel)** encontrarse mal
in dentro
include v incluir
indoor pool la piscina cubierta
inexpensive barato
infected infectado
information (phone) el número de teléfono de información; **~ desk** el mostrador de información
insect el insecto; **~ bite** la picadura de insecto; **~ repellent** el repelente de insectos
insert v introducir
insomnia el insomnio
instant message el mensaje instantáneo
insulin la insulina
insurance el seguro; **~ card** la tarjeta de seguro; **~ company** la compañia de seguros
interesting interesante
intermediate el nivel intermedio
international (airport area) internacional; **~ flight** el vuelo internacional; **~ student card** la tarjeta internacional de estudiante
internet la internet; **~ cafe** el cibercafé; **~**

service el servicio de internet; **wireless ~** el acceso inalámbrico
interpreter el/la intérprete
intersection el cruce
intestine el intestino
introduce v presentar
invoice [BE] la factura
Ireland Irlanda
Irish irlandés
iron v planchar; **~** n **(clothes)** la plancha
Italian italiano

J

jacket la chaqueta
jar el bote
jaw la mandíbula
jazz el jazz; **~ club** el club de jazz
jeans los vaqueros
jet ski la moto acuática
jeweler la joyería
jewelry las joyas
join v acompañar a
joint (body part) la articulación

K

key la llave; **~ card** la llave electrónica; **~ ring** el llavero
kiddie pool la piscina infantil
kidney (body part) el riñón
kilo el kilo; **~gram** el kilogramo; **~meter** el kilómetro
kiss v besar
kitchen la cocina; **~**

foil [BE] el papel de aluminio
knee la rodilla
knife el cuchillo

L

lace el encaje
lactose intolerant alérgico a la lactosa
lake el lago
large grande; **~er** más grande
last último
late (time) tarde; **~er** más tarde
launderette [BE] la lavandería
laundromat la lavandería
laundry la colada; **~ facility** la lavandería; **~ service** el servicio de lavandería
lawyer el abogado
leather el cuero
to leave v salir
left (direction) la izquierda
leg la pierna
lens la lente
less menos
lesson la lección
letter la carta
library la biblioteca
life la vida; **~ jacket** el chaleco salvavidas; **~guard** el socorrista
lift n [BE] el ascensor; **~** v **(to give a ride)** llevar en coche; **~ pass** el pase de acceso a los remontes

DICTIONARY

light n (overhead) la luz; ~ v (cigarette) dar fuego; ~**bulb** la bombilla
lighter el mechero
like v gustar; **I like** me gusta
line (train) la línea
linen el lino
lip el labio
liquor store la tienda de bebidas alcohólicas
liter el litro
little pequeño
live v vivir
liver (body part) el hígado
loafers los mocasines
local de la zona
lock v cerrar; ~ n el cerrojo
locker la taquilla
log on v (computer) iniciar sesión
log off v (computer) cerrar sesión
long largo; ~ **sleeves** las mangas largas; ~**sighted** [BE] hipermétrope
look v mirar
lose v (something) perder
lost perdido; ~ **and found** la oficina de objetos perdidos
lotion la crema hidratante
louder más alto
love v querer; ~ n el amor
low bajo; ~**er** más bajo

luggage el equipaje; ~ **cart** el carrito de equipaje; ~ **locker** la consigna automática; ~ **ticket** el talón de equipaje; **hand** ~ [BE] el equipaje de mano
lunch la comida
lung el pulmón

M

magazine la revista
magnificent magnífico
mail v enviar por correo; ~ n el correo; ~**box** el buzón de correo
main principal; ~ **attractions** los principales sitios de interés; ~ **course** el plato principal
make up a prescription v [BE] despachar medicamentos
mall el centro comercial
man el hombre
manager el gerente
manicure la manicura
manual car el coche con transmisión manual
map el mapa
market el mercado
married casado
marry v casarse
mass (church service) la misa
massage el masaje
match la cerilla
meal la comida

measure v (someone) medir
measuring cup la taza medidora
measuring spoon la cuchara medidora
mechanic el mecánico
medicine el medicamento
medium (size) mediano
meet v (someone) conocer
meeting la reunión; ~ **room** la sala de reuniones
membership card la tarjeta de socio
memorial (place) el monumento conmemorativo
memory card la tarjeta de memoria
mend v zurcir
menstrual cramps los dolores menstruales
menu la carta
message el mensaje
meter (parking) el parquímetro
microwave el microondas
midday [BE] el mediodía
midnight la medianoche
mileage el kilometraje
mini-bar el minibar
minute el minuto
missing desaparecido
mistake el error
mobile móvil; ~ **home** la caravana; ~ **phone** [BE] el teléfono móvil

mobility la movilidad
money el dinero
month el mes
mop la fregona
moped el ciclomotor
more más
morning la mañana
mosque la mezquita
mother la madre
motion sickness el mareo
motor el motor; ~ **boat** la lancha motora; ~**cycle** la motocicleta; ~**way** [BE] la autopista
mountain la montaña; ~ **bike** la bicicleta de montaña
mousse (hair) la espuma para el pelo
mouth n la boca
movie la película; ~ **theater** el cine
mug v asaltar
muscle (body part) el músculo
museum el museo
music la música; ~ **store** la tienda de música

N

nail la uña; ~ **file** la lima de uñas; ~ **salon** el salón de manicura
name el nombre
napkin la servilleta
nappy [BE] el pañale
nationality la nacionalidad
nature preserve la reserva natural

(be) nauseous v tener náuseas
near cerca; **~-sighted** miope; **~by** cerca de aquí
neck el cuello
necklace el collar
need v necesitar
newspaper el periódico
newsstand el quiosco
next próximo
nice adj amable
night la noche; **~club** la discoteca
no no
non adj; **~-alcoholic** sin alcohol; **~-smoking** para no fumadores
noon el mediodía
north el norte
nose la nariz
note [BE] el billete
nothing nada
notify v avisar
novice (skill level) principiante
now ahora
number el número
nurse el enfermero/la enfermera

O

office la oficina; **~ hours (doctor's)** las horas de consulta; **~ hours (other offices)** el horario de oficina
off-licence [BE] la tienda de bebidas alcohólicas
oil el aceite
OK de acuerdo

old adj viejo
on the corner en la esquina
once una vez
one uno; **~-way ticket** el billete de ida; **~-way street** la calle de sentido único
only solamente
open v abrir; **~** adj abierto
opera la ópera; **~-house** el teatro de la ópera
opposite frente a
optician el oculista
orange (color) naranja
orchestra la orquesta
order v pedir
outdoor pool la piscina exterior
outside fuera
over sobre; **~ the counter (medication)** sin receta; **~-look (scenic place)** el mirador; **~night** por la noche
oxygen treatment la oxigenoterapia

P

p.m. de la tarde
pacifier el chupete
pack v hacer las maletas
package el paquete
paddling pool [BE] la piscina infantil
pad [BE] la compresa
pain el dolor
pajamas los pijamas
palace el palacio

pants los pantalones
pantyhose las medias
paper el papel; **~ towel** el papel de cocina
paracetamol [BE] el paracetamol
park v aparcar; **~** n el parque; **~ing garage** el párking; **~ing lot** el aparcamiento
parliament building el palacio de las cortes
part (for car) la pieza; **~-time** a tiempo parcial
pass through v estar de paso
passenger el pasajero
passport el pasaporte; **~ control** el control de pasaportes
password la contraseña
pastry shop la pastelería
path el camino
pay v pagar; **~ phone** el teléfono público
peak (of a mountain) la cima
pearl la perla
pedestrian el peatón
pediatrician el pediatra
pedicure la pedicura
pen el bolígrafo
penicillin la penicilina
penis el pene
per por; **~ day** por día; **~ hour** por hora; **~ night** por

noche; **~ week** por semana
perfume el perfume
period (menstrual) la regla; **~ (of time)** la época
permit v permitir
petite las tallas pequeñas
petrol la gasolina; **~ station** la gasolinera
pewter el peltre
pharmacy la farmacia
phone v hacer una llamada; **~** n el teléfono; **~ call** la llamada de teléfono; **~ card** la tarjeta telefónica; **~ number** el número de teléfono
photo la foto; **~-copy** la fotocopia; **~graphy** la fotografía
pick up v (something) recoger
picnic area la zona para picnic
piece el trozo
Pill (birth control) la píldora
pillow la almohada
personal identification number (PIN) la clave
pink rosa
piste [BE] la pista; **~ map [BE]** el mapa de pistas
pizzeria la pizzería
place v (a bet) hacer una apuesta
plane el avión

plastic wrap el film transparente
plate el plato
platform [BE] (train) el andén
platinum el platino
play v jugar; ~ n (theater) la obra de teatro; **~ground** el patio de recreo; **~pen** el parque
please por favor
pleasure el placer
plunger el desatascador
plus size la talla grande
pocket el bolsillo
poison el veneno
poles (skiing) los bastones
police la policía; **~ report** el certificado de la policía; **~ station** la comisaría
pond el estanque
pool la piscina
pop music la música pop
portion la ración
post [BE] el correo; **~office** la oficina de correos; **~box [BE]** el buzón de correos; **~card** la tarjeta postal
pot la olla
pottery la cerámica
pounds (British sterling) las libras esterlinas
pregnant embarazada
prescribe v recetar
prescription la receta
press v **(clothing)** planchar
price el precio
print v imprimir
problem el problema
produce las frutas y verduras; **~ store** la frutería y verdulería
prohibit v prohibir
pronounce v pronunciar
public el público
pull v **(door sign)** tirar
purple morado
purse el bolso
push v **(door sign)** empujar; **~chair [BE]** el cochecito de niño

Q

quality n la calidad
question la pregunta
quiet adj tranquilo

R

racetrack el circuito de carreras
racket (sports) la raqueta
railway station [BE] la estación de trenes
rain la lluvia; **~coat** el chubasquero; **~forest** el bosque pluvial; **~y** adv lluvioso
rap (music) el rap
rape v violar; ~ n la violación
rash la erupción cutánea
razor blade la hoja de afeitar

reach v localizar
ready listo
real auténtico
receipt el recibo
receive v recibir
reception la recepción
recharge v recargar
recommend v recomendar
recommendation la recomendación
recycle v reciclar
red rojo
refrigerator n la nevera
region la región
registered mail el correo certificado
regular normal
relationship la relación
rent v alquilar
rental car el coche de alquiler
repair v arreglar
repeat v repetir
reservation la reserva; **~ desk** la taquilla
reserve v reservar
restaurant el restaurante
restroom el servicio
retired jubilado
return v **(something)** devolver; ~ n **[BE]** la ida y vuelta
rib (body part) la costilla
right (direction) derecha; **~ of way** prioridad de paso
ring el anillo
river n el río
road map el mapa de carreteras

rob v atracar
robbed atracado
romantic romántico
room la habitación; **~ key** la llave de habitación; **~ service** el servicio de habitaciones
round-trip ida y vuelta
route la ruta
rowboat la barca de remos
rubbish [BE] la basura; **~ bag [BE]** la bolsa de basura
rugby el rugby
ruins las ruinas
rush la prisa

S

sad triste
safe n la caja fuerte; ~ adj seguro
sales tax el IVA
same mismo
sandals las sandalias
sanitary napkin la compresa
saucepan el cazo
sauna la sauna
save v **(computer)** guardar
savings (account) la cuenta de ahorro
scanner el escáner
scarf la bufanda
schedule v programar; ~ n el horario
school el colegio
science la ciencia
scissors las tijeras
sea el mar
seat el asiento
security la seguridad
see v ver

DICTIONARY

self-service el autoservicio
sell v vender
seminar el seminario
send v enviar
senior citizen jubilado
separated (marriage) -separado
serious serio
service (in a restaurant) el servicio
sexually transmitted disease (STD) la enfermedad de transmisión sexual
shampoo el champú
sharp afilado
shaving cream la crema de afeitar
sheet la sábana
ship v enviar
shirt la camisa
shoe store la zapatería
shoes los zapatos
shop v comprar
shopping ir de compras; **~ area** la zona de compras; **~ centre [BE]** el centro comercial; **~ mall** el centro comercial
short corto; **~ sleeves** las mangas cortas; **~s** los pantalones cortos; **~-sighted [BE]** miope
shoulder el hombro
show v enseñar
shower la ducha
shrine el santuario
sick enfermo
side el lado; **~ dish** la guarnición; **~ effect** el efecto secundario; **~ order** la guarnición
sightsee v hacer turismo
sightseeing tour el recorrido turístico
sign v **(name)** firmar
silk la seda
silver la plata
single (unmarried) soltero; **~ bed** la cama; **~ prints** una copia; **~ room** una habitación individual
sink el lavabo
sister la hermana
sit v sentarse
size la talla
skin la piel
skirt la falda
ski v esquiar; **~ n** el esquí; **~ lift** el telesquí
sleep v dormir; **~er car** el coche cama; **~ing bag** el saco de dormir
slice v cortar en rodajas
slippers las zapatillas
slower más despacio
slowly despacio
small pequeño
smaller más pequeño
smoke v fumar
smoking (area) la zona de fumadores
snack bar la cafetería
sneakers las zapatillas de deporte
snorkeling equipment el equipo de esnórquel
snow la nieve; **~board** la tabla de snowboard; **~shoe** la raqueta de nieve; **~y** nevado
soap el jabón
soccer el fútbol
sock el calcetín
some alguno
soother [BE] el chupete
sore throat las anginas
sorry lo siento
south el sur
souvenir el recuerdo; **~ store** la tienda de recuerdos
spa el centro de salud y belleza
Spain España
Spanish el español
spatula la espátula
speak v hablar
special (food) la especialidad de la casa
specialist (doctor) el especialista
specimen el ejemplar
speeding el exceso de velocidad
spell v deletrear
spicy picante
spine (body part) la columna vertebral
spoon la cuchara
sports los deportes; **~ massage** el masaje deportivo
sporting goods store la tienda de deportes
sprain el esguince
square cuadrado; **~ kilometer** el kilómetro cuadrado; **~ meter** el metro cuadrado
stadium el estadio
stairs las escaleras
stamp v **(a ticket)** picar; **~ n (postage)** el sello
start v empezar
starter [BE] el aperitivo
station la estación; **bus ~** la estación de autobuses; **gas ~** la gasolinera; **muster ~ [BE]** el punto de reunión; **petrol ~ [BE]** la gasolinera; **subway ~** el metro; **train ~** la estación de tren
statue la estatua
stay v quedarse
steal v robar
steep empinado
sterling silver la plata esterlina
sting el escozor
stolen robado
stomach el estómago; **~ache** el dolor de estómago
stop v pararse; **~ n** la parada
storey [BE] la planta
stove el horno
straight recto
strange extraño
stream el arroyo
stroller el cochecito
student el estudiante
study v estudiar
stunning impresionante

DICTIONARY

subtitle el subtítulo
subway el metro; **~ station** la estación de metro
suit el traje
suitcase la maleta
sun el sol; **~block** el protector solar total; **~burn** la quemadura solar; **~glasses** las gafas de sol; **~ny** soleado; **~screen** el protector solar; **~stroke** la insolación
super (fuel) súper; **~market** el supermercado
surfboard la tabla de surf
surgical spirit [BE] el alcohol etílico
swallow v tragar
sweater el jersey
sweatshirt la sudadera
sweet (taste) dulce; **~s [BE]** los caramelos
swelling la hinchazón
swim v nadar; **~suit** el bañador
symbol (keyboard) el símbolo
synagogue la sinagoga

T

table la mesa
tablet (medicine) el comprimido
take v llevar; **~ away [BE]** para llevar
tampon el tampón
tapas bar el bar de tapas
taste v probar
taxi el taxi
team el equipo
telephone el teléfono
temporary provisional
tennis el tenis
tent la tienda de campaña; **~ peg** la estaca; **~ pole** el mástil
terminal (airport) la terminal
terracotta la terracotta
terrible terrible
text v **(send a message)** enviar un mensaje de texto; **~** n **(message)** el texto
thank v dar las gracias a; **~ you** gracias
that eso
theater el teatro
there ahí
thief el ladrón
thigh el muslo
thirsty sediento
this esto
throat la garganta
ticket el billete; **~ office** el despacho de billetes; **~ed passenger** el pasajero con billete
tie (clothing) la corbata
time el tiempo; **~table [BE]** el horario
tire la rueda
tired cansado
tissue el pañuelo de papel
tobacconist el estanco

today hoy
toe el dedo del pie; **~nail** la uña del pie
toilet [BE] el servicio; **~ paper** el papel higiénico
tomorrow mañana
tongue la lengua
tonight esta noche
too demasiado
tooth el diente; **~brush** el cepillo de dientes; **~paste** la pasta de dientes
total (amount) el total
tough (food) duro
tourist el turista; **~ information office** la oficina de turismo
tour el recorrido turístico
tow truck la grúa
towel la toalla
tower la torre
town la ciudad; **~ hall** el ayuntamiento; **~ map** el mapa de ciudad; **~ square** la plaza
toy el juguete; **~ store** la tienda de juguetes
track (train) el andén
traditional tradicional
traffic light el semáforo
trail la pista; **~ map** el mapa de la pista
trailer el remolque
train el tren; **~ station** la estación de tren
transfer v cambiar

translate v traducir
trash la basura
travel v viajar; **~ agency** la agencia de viajes; **~ sickness** el mareo; **~er's check [cheque BE]** el cheque de viaje
tree el árbol
trim (hair cut) cortarse las puntas
trip el viaje
trolley [BE] el carrito
trousers [BE] los pantalones
T-shirt la camiseta
turn off v apagar
turn on v encender
TV la televisión
type v escribir a máquina
tyre [BE] la rueda

U

United Kingdom (U.K.) el Reino Unido
United States (U.S.) los Estados Unidos
ugly feo
umbrella el paraguas
unattended desatendido
unconscious inconsciente
underground [BE] el metro; **~ station [BE]** la estación de metro
underpants [BE] los calzoncillos
understand v entender
underwear la ropa interior

153

DICTIONARY

university la universidad
unleaded (gas) la gasolina sin plomo
upper superior
urgent urgente
use v usar
username el nombre de usuario
utensil el cubierto

V

vacancy la habitación libre
vacation las vacaciones
vaccination la vacuna
vacuum cleaner la aspiradora
vaginal infection la infección vaginal
valid validez
valley el valle
valuable valioso
VAT [BE] el IVA
vegetarian vegetariano
vehicle registration el registro del coche
viewpoint [BE] el mirador
village el pueblo
vineyard la viña
visa (passport document) el visado
visit v visitar; **~ing hours** el horario de visita
visually impaired la persona con discapacidad visual
vitamin la vitamina
V-neck el cuello de pico
vomit v vomitar

W

wait v esperar; **~** n la espera; **~ing room** la sala de espera
waiter el camarero
waitress la camarera
wake v despertarse; **~-up call** la llamada despertador
walk v caminar; **~** n la caminata; **~ing route** la ruta de senderismo
wallet la cartera
warm v (something) calentar; **~** adj (temperature) calor

washing machine la lavadora
watch el reloj
waterfall la cascada
weather el tiempo
week la semana; **~end** el fin de semana; **~ly** semanal
welcome v acoger
well bien; **~-rested** descansado
west el oeste
what (question) qué
wheelchair la silla de ruedas; **~ ramp** la rampa para silla de ruedas
when (question) cuándo
where (question) dónde
white blanco; **~ gold** el oro blanco
who (question) quién
widowed viudo
wife la mujer
window la ventana; **~ case** el escaparate
windsurfer el surfista
wine list la carta de vinos

wireless inalámbrico; **~ internet** el acceso inalámbrico a internet; **~ internet service** el servicio inalámbrico a internet; **~ phone** el teléfono móvil
with con
withdraw v retirar; **~al (bank)** retirar fondos
without sin
woman la mujer
wool la lana
work v trabajar
wrap v envolver
wrist la muñeca
write v escribir

Y

year el año
yellow amarillo
yes sí
yesterday ayer
young joven
youth hostel el albergue juvenil

Z

zoo el zoológico

SPANISH-ENGLISH

A

a tiempo completo full-time
a tiempo parcial part-time
la abadía abbey
el abanico fan (souvenir)
abierto adj open
el abogado lawyer
abrazar v hug
el abrebotellas bottle opener
el abrelatas can opener
el abrigo coat
abrir v open
el abuelo grandparent
aburrido boring
acampar v camp
el acantilado cliff
el acceso access; **~ inalámbrico a internet** wireless internet; **~ para discapacitados** handicapped- [disabled-BE] accessible
el accidente accident
el aceite oil
aceptar v accept
acoger v welcome

DICTIONARY

acompañar a v join
la acupuntura acupuncture
el adaptador adapter
adicional extra
adiós goodbye
las aduanas customs
el aeropuerto airport
afilado sharp
la agencia agency; **~ de viajes** travel agency
agotado exhausted
el agua water; **~ caliente** hot water; **~ potable** drinking water
las aguas termales hot spring
ahí there
ahora now
el aire air, air pump; **~ acondicionado** air conditioning
el albergue hostel; **~ juvenil** youth hostel
alérgico allergic; **~ a la lactosa** lactose intolerant
algo anything
el algodón cotton
alguno some
alimentar v feed
el allanamiento de morada break-in (burglary)
la almohada pillow
el alojamiento accommodation
alquilar v rent [hire BE]; **el ~ de coches** car rental [hire BE]
alto high

amable nice
amarillo yellow
la ambulancia ambulance
el amigo friend
el amor n love
el andén track [platform BE] (train)
anémico anemic
la anestesia anesthesia
las anginas sore throat
el anillo ring
el animal animal
antes de before
el antibiótico antibiotic
el año year
apagar v turn off
el aparcamiento parking lot [car park BE]
aparcar v park
el apartamento apartment
el apéndice appendix (body part)
el aperitivo appetizer [starter BE]
aquí here
el árbol tree
la aromaterapia aromatherapy
el arroyo stream
arreglar v repair
la arteria artery
la articulación joint (body part)
los artículos goods; **~ para el hogar** household good
la artritis arthritis
asaltar v mug
el asalto attack

el ascensor elevator [lift BE]
asiático Asian
el asiento seat; **~ de niño** car seat; **~ de pasillo** aisle seat
asistir v attend
asmático asthmatic
la aspiradora vacuum cleaner
la aspirina aspirin
atracado robbed
atracar v rob
Australia Australia
australiano Australian
auténtico real
el autobús bus; **~ rápido** express bus
automático automatic
la autopista highway [motorway BE]
el autoservicio self-service
la avería breakdown
el avión airplane, plane
avisar v notify
ayer yesterday
la ayuda n help
ayudar v help
el ayuntamiento town hall
azul blue

B

bailar v dance
bajarse v get off (a train, bus, subway)
bajo low
el ballet ballet
el baloncesto basketball
el bálsamo para después del afeitado aftershave

el banco bank
el bañador swimsuit
el baño bathroom
el bar bar; **~ de tapas** tapas bar; **~ gay** gay bar
barato cheap, inexpensive
la barbacoa barbecue
la barca de remos rowboat
el barco boat
los bastones poles (skiing)
la basura trash [rubbish BE]
la batería battery (car)
el bebé baby
beber v drink
la bebida n drink
beis beige
el béisbol baseball
besar v kiss
el biberón baby bottle
la biblioteca library
la bicicleta bicycle; **~ de montaña** mountain bike
el billete n bill (money); ~ ticket; **~ de autobús** bus ticket; **~ de ida** one-way (ticket); **~ de ida y vuelta** round trip [return BE]; **~ electrónico** e-ticket
el biquini bikini
blanco white
la blusa blouse
la boca mouth
el bolígrafo pen
la bolsa de basura garbage [rubbish BE] bag

155

156 DICTIONARY

el bolsillo pocket
el bolso purse [handbag BE]
los bomberos fire department
la bombilla lightbulb
borrar v clear (on an ATM); ~ v delete (computer)
el bosque forest; ~ **pluvial** rainforest
las botas boots; ~ **de montaña** hiking boots
el bote jar
la botella bottle
el brazo arm
británico British
el broche brooch
bucear to dive
bueno adj good
buenas noches good evening
buenas tardes good afternoon
buenos días good morning
la bufanda scarf
el buzón de correo mailbox [postbox BE]

C

la cabaña cabin (house)
el cabaré cabaret
la cabeza head (body part)
la cafetería cafe, coffee shop, snack bar
la caja case (amount); ~ **fuerte** n safe
el cajero cashier; ~ **automático** ATM
el calcetín sock

la calefacción heater [heating BE]
calentar v heat, warm
la calidad quality
la calle de sentido único one-way street
calor hot, warm (temperature)
las calorías calories
los calzoncillos briefs [underpants BE] (clothing)
la cama single bed; ~ **de matrimonio** double bed
la cámara camera; ~ **digital** digital camera
la camarera waitress
el camarero waiter
el camarote cabin (ship)
cambiar v change, exchange, transfer
el cambio n change (money); ~ **de divisas** currency exchange
caminar v walk
la caminata n walk
el camino path
la camisa shirt
la camiseta T-shirt
el cámping campsite
el campo field (sports); ~ **de batalla** battleground; ~ **de golf** golf course
Canadá Canada
canadiense Canadian
cancelar v cancel
el/la canguro babysitter

cansado tired
el cañón canyon
la cara face
los caramelos candy [sweets BE]
la caravana mobile home
el carbón charcoal
el carnicero butcher
caro expensive
el carrete film (camera)
el carrito cart [trolley BE] (grocery store); ~ **de equipaje** luggage cart
la carta letter
la carta n menu; ~ **de bebidas** drink menu; ~ **para niños** children's menu; ~ **de vinos** wine list
la cartera n wallet
el cartón carton; ~ **de tabaco** carton of cigarettes
la casa house; ~ **de cambio** currency exchange office
casado married
casarse v marry
la cascada waterfall
el casco helmet
los cascos headphones
el casino casino
el castillo castle
el catarro cold (sickness)
la catedral cathedral
el catre cot
causar daño v damage
el cazo saucepan
el CD CD

la cena dinner
el centímetro centimeter
el centro downtown area; ~ **comercial** shopping mall [centre BE]; ~ **de negocios** business center; ~ **de salud y belleza** spa
el cepillo de pelo hair brush
la cerámica pottery
cerca near; ~ **de aquí** nearby
la cerilla n match
cerrado closed
cerrar v close, lock; ~ **sesión** v log off (computer)
el cerrojo n lock
el certificado certificate; ~ **de la policía** police report
la cesta basket (grocery store)
el chaleco salvavidas life jacket
el champú shampoo
la chaqueta jacket
la charcutería delicatessen
el cheque n check [cheque BE] (payment); ~ **de viaje** traveler's check [cheque BE]
el chicle chewing gum
chino Chinese
el chubasquero raincoat
el chupete pacifier [soother BE]

DICTIONARY

el cibercafé internet cafe
el ciclismo cycling
el ciclomotor moped
la ciencia science
el cigarrillo cigarette
la cima peak (of a mountain)
el cine movie theater
la cinta transportadora conveyor belt
el cinturón n belt
el circuito de carreras racetrack
la cita appointment
la ciudad town
la clase class; **~ económica** economy class; **~ preferente** business class
la clave personal identification number (PIN)
el club de jazz jazz club
cobrar v bill (charge); **~** v cash; **~** v charge (credit card)
el cobre copper
el coche n car; **~ de alquiler** rental [hire BE] car; **~ automático** automatic car; **~ cama** sleeper [sleeping BE] car; **~ con transmisión manual** manual car
el cochecito stroller [pushchair BE]
la cocina kitchen
cocinar v cook
el código de país country code
el codo elbow

la colada laundry
el colegio school
la colina hill
el collar necklace
la colonia cologne
el color color
la columna vertebral spine (body part)
el comedor dining room
comer v eat
la comida food, lunch, meal; **~ rápida** fast food
la comisaría police station
cómo how
el compañero de trabajo colleague
la compañía company; **~ aérea** airline; **~ de seguros** insurance company
comprar v buy, shop
la compresa sanitary napkin [pad BE]
el comprimido tablet (medicine)
con with; **~ plomo** leaded (gas)
el concierto concert
conducir v drive
conectarse v connect (internet)
la conexión connection (internet); **~ de vuelo** connection (flight)
la conferencia conference
confirmar v confirm
el congelador freezer
la congestión congestion

conocer v meet (someone)
la consigna automática luggage locker
el consulado Consulate
el consultor consultant
contagioso contagious
la contraseña password
el control de pasaportes passport control
el corazón heart
la corbata tie (clothing)
el correo n mail [post BE]; **~ aéreo** airmail; **~ certificado** registered mail; **~ electrónico** n e-mail
cortar v cut (hair); **~ en rodajas** to slice
cortarse las puntas v trim (hair cut)
el corte n cut (injury); **~ de pelo** haircut
corto short
costar v cost
la costilla rib (body part)
la crema cream; **~ antiséptica** antiseptic cream; **~ de afeitar** shaving cream; **~ hidratante** lotion
el cristal crystal
el cruce intersection
cuándo when (question)
cuánto cuesta how

much
el cubierto utensil
la cuchara spoon; **~ medidora** measuring spoon
la cucharadita teaspoon
la cuchilla desechable disposable razor
el cuchillo knife
el cuello neck; **~ de pico** V-neck; **~ redondo** crew neck
el cuenco bowl
la cuenta account; **~ de ahorro** savings account; **~ corriente** checking [current BE] account
cuero leather
la cueva cave
el cumpleaños birthday
la cuna crib

D

dar to give; **~ el pecho** breastfeed; **~ fuego** light (cigarette); **~ las gracias** v thank
de from, of; **~ acuerdo** OK; **~ la mañana** a.m.; **~ la tarde** p.m.; **~ la zona** local
declarar v declare
el dedo finger; **~ del pie** toe
deletrear v spell
delicioso delicious
la dentadura denture
el dentista dentist
dentro in

157

la depilacion wax; **~ de cejas** eyebrow wax; **~ de las ingles** bikini wax
deportes sports
depositar v deposit
el depósito bancario deposit (bank)
la derecha right (direction)
desaparecido missing
el desatascador plunger
desatendido unattended
el desayuno breakfast
descansado well-rested
desconectar v disconnect (computer)
el descuento discount
desechable disposable
el desierto desert
el desodorante deodorant
despachar medicamentos v fill (make up BE) a prescription
el despacho de billetes ticket office
despacio slowly
despertarse v wake
después after
el detergente detergent
detrás de behind (direction)
devolver v exchange, return (goods)
el día day
diabético diabetic
el diamante diamond
la diarrea diarrhea
el diente tooth

el diesel diesel
difícil difficult
digital digital
el dinero money
la dirección direction
la dirección address; **~ de correo electrónico** e-mail address
discapacitado handicapped [disabled BE]
la discoteca club (dance, night); **~ gay** gay club
disculparse v excuse (to get attention)
disfrutar v enjoy
disponible available
divorciar v divorce
doblada dubbed
doblando (la esquina) around (the corner)
la docena dozen
el documento de identidad identification
el dólar dollar (U.S.)
el dolor pain; **~ de cabeza** headache; **~ de espalda** backache; **~ de estómago** stomachache; **~ de oído** earache; **~ de pecho** chest pain
los dolores menstruales menstrual cramps
dónde where (question)
dormir v sleep
el dormitorio dormitory
la ducha shower

dulce sweet (taste)
durante during
el DVD DVD

E

la edad age
el edificio building
el efectivo cash
el efecto secundario side effect
el ejemplar specimen
embarazada pregnant
embarcar v board
la emergencia emergency
el empaste filling (tooth)
empezar v begin, start
empinado steep
empujar v push (door sign)
en la esquina on the corner
el encaje lace
encender v turn on
el enchufe eléctrico electric outlet
encontrarse mal v be ill
la enfermedad de transmisión sexual sexually transmitted disease (STD)
el enfermero/la enfermera nurse
enfermo sick
enseñar v show
entender v understand
la entrada admission/cover charge; **~** entrance
entrar v enter
el entretenimiento entertainment

enviar v send, ship; **~ por correo** v mail; **~ un correo electrónico** v e-mail; **~ un fax** v fax; **~ un mensaje de texto** v text (send a message)
envolver v wrap
la época period (of time)
el equipaje luggage [baggage BE]; **~ de mano** carry-on (piece of hand luggage)
el equipo team
el equipo equipment; **~ de buceo** diving equipment; **~ de esnórquel** snorkeling equipment
equis ele (XL) extra large
el error mistake
la erupción cutánea rash
las escaleras stairs; **~ mecánicas** escalators
el escáner scanner
el escaparate window case
la escoba broom
el escozor sting
escribir v write; **~ a máquina** v type
el escurridor colander
el esguince sprain
el esmalte enamel (jewelry)
eso that
la espalda back
España Spain
el español Spanish

DICTIONARY

la espátula spatula
la especialidad de la casa special (food)
la especialista specialist (doctor)
la espera n wait
esperar v wait
la espuma para el pelo mousse (hair)
el esquí n ski
esquiar v ski
los esquís acuáticos water skis
esta noche tonight
la estaca tent peg
la estación station; ~ de autobuses bus station; ~ de metro subway [underground BE] station; ~ de tren train [railway BE] station
el estadio stadium
el estado de salud condition (medical)
los Estados Unidos United States (U.S.)
estadounidense American
el estanco tobacconist
el estanque pond
estar v be; ~ de paso v pass through
la estatua statue
el este east
el estilista hairstylist
esto this
el estómago stomach
estrellarse v crash (car)
estreñido constipated
estudiando studying
el estudiante student

estudiar v study
el euro euro
el exceso excess; ~ de velocidad speeding
la excursión excursion
experto expert (skill level)
la extensión extension (phone)
extraer v extract (tooth)
extraño strange

F
fácil adj easy
la factura bill [invoice BE]
la facturación check-in (airport)
facturar check (luggage)
la falda skirt
la familia family
la farmacia pharmacy [chemist BE]
el fax n fax
la fecha date (calendar)
feliz adj happy
feo adj ugly
el ferry ferry
la fianza deposit (to reserve a room)
la fiebre fever
el film transparente plastic wrap [cling film BE]
el fin de semana weekend
firmar v sign (name)
la flor flower
la fórmula infantil formula (baby)
el formulario form

la foto exposure (film); ~ photo; ~copia photocopy; ~grafía photography; ~ digital digital photo
la fregona mop
los frenos brakes (car)
frente a opposite
fresco fresh
frío adj cold (temperature)
las frutas y verduras produce
la frutería y verdulería produce store
el fuego fire
la fuente fountain
fuera outside
el fuerte fort
fumar v smoke
la funda para la cámara camera case
el fútbol soccer [football BE]

G
las gafas glasses; ~ de sol sunglasses
el garaje garage (parking)
la garganta throat
la garrafa carafe
el gas butano cooking gas
la gasolina gas [petrol BE]; ~ sin plomo unleaded gas
la gasolinera gas [petrol BE] station
gay gay
el gerente manager
el gimnasio gym
el ginecólogo gynecologist

la gomina gel (hair)
la gota drop (medicine)
grabar v burn (CD); ~ v engrave
gracias thank you
los grados degrees (temperature); ~ centígrado Celsius
el gramo gram
grande large
los grandes almacenes department store
la granja farm
gratuito free
gris gray
la grúa tow truck
el grupo group
guapo attractive
guardar v save (computer)
la guarnición side dish, order
la guía guide
la guía guide book; ~ de tiendas store directory
gustar v like; me gusta I like

H
ha sufrido daños damaged
la habitación room; ~ individual single room; ~ libre vacancy
hablar v speak
hacer v do; ~ una apuesta v place (a bet); ~ un arreglo v alter; ~ una llamada v phone; ~ las maletas v pack; ~ turismo sightseeing

hambriento hungry
helado icy
la hermana sister
el hermano brother
el hielo ice
el hígado liver (body part)
la hinchazón swelling
hipermétrope far-sighted [long-sighted BE]
el hipódromo horse-track
el hockey hockey; **~ sobre hielo** ice hockey
la hoja de afeitar razor blade
hola hello
el hombre man
el hombro shoulder
hondo deeply
la hora hour
el horario n schedule [timetable BE]
los horarios hours; **~ de atención al público** business hours; **~ de oficina** office hours; **~ de visita** visiting hours
las horas de consulta office hours (doctor's)
el hornillo camp stove
el horno stove
el hospital hospital
el hotel hotel
hoy today
el hueso bone

I

el ibuprofeno ibuprofen
la ida y vuelta round-trip [return BE]
la iglesia church
impresionante stunning
imprimir v print
el impuesto duty (tax)
incluir v include
inconsciente unconscious
increíble amazing
la infección vaginal vaginal infection
infectado infected
el inglés English
iniciar sesión v log on (computer)
el insecto bug
la insolación sunstroke
el insomnio insomnia
la insulina insulin
interesante interesting
internacional international (airport area)
la internet internet
el/la intérprete interpreter
el intestino intestine
introducir v insert
ir a v go (somewhere)
ir de compras v go shopping
Irlanda Ireland
irlandés Irish
el IVA sales tax [VAT BE]
la izquierda left (direction)

J

el jabón soap
el jardín botánico botanical garden
el jazz jazz
el jersey sweater
joven young
las joyas jewelry
la joyería jeweler
jubilado retired
jugar v play
el juguete toy

K

el kilo kilo; **~gramo** kilogram; **~metraje** mileage
el kilómetro kilometer; **~ cuadrado** square kilometer

L

el labio lip
la laca hairspray
el ladrón thief
el lago lake
la lana wool
la lancha motora motor boat
largo long
el lavabo sink
la lavadora washing machine
la lavandería laundromat [launderette BE]
lavar v wash
el lavavajillas dishwasher
la lección lesson
lejos far
la lengua tongue
la lente lens
las lentillas de contacto contact lens
las letras arts
las libras esterlinas pounds (British sterling)
libre de impuestos duty-free

la librería bookstore
el libro book
la lima de uñas nail file
limpiar v clean
la limpieza de cutis facial
limpio adj clean
la línea line (train)
el lino linen
la linterna flashlight
el líquido liquid; **~ de lentillas de contacto** contact lens solution; **~ lavavajillas** dishwashing liquid
listo ready
la litera berth
el litro liter
la llamada n call; **~ de teléfono** phone call; **~ despertador** wake-up call
llamar v call
la llave key; **~ de habitación** room key; **~ electrónica** key card
el llavero key ring
las llegadas arrivals (airport)
llegar v arrive
llenar v fill
llevar v take; **~ en coche** lift (to give a ride)
la lluvia rain
lluvioso rainy
lo siento sorry
localizar v reach
la luz light (overhead)

M

la madre mother
magnífico magnificent

DICTIONARY

el malestar estomacal upset stomach
la maleta bag, suitcase
la mandíbula jaw
las mangas cortas short sleeves
las mangas largas long sleeves
la manicura manicure
la mano hand
la manta blanket
mañana tomorrow; **la ~** morning
el mapa map; **~ de carreteras** road map; **~ de ciudad** town map; **~ de la pista** trail [piste BE] map
el mar sea
marcar v dial
mareado dizzy
el mareo motion [travel BE] sickness
el marido husband
marrón brown
el martillo hammer
más more; **~ alto** louder; **~ bajo** lower; **~ barato** cheaper; **~ despacio** slower; **~ grande** larger; **~ pequeño** smaller; **~ rápido** faster; **~ tarde** later; **~ temprano** earlier
el masaje massage; **~ deportivo** sports massage
el mástil tent pole
el mecánico mechanic
el mechero lighter
la media hora half hour

mediano medium (size)
la medianoche midnight
el medicamento medicine
el médico doctor
medio half; **~ kilo** half-kilo; **~día** noon [midday BE]
medir v measure (someone)
mejor best
menos less
el mensaje message; **~ instantáneo** instant message
el mercado market
el mes month
la mesa table
el metro subway [underground BE]
el metro cuadrado square meter
la mezquita mosque
el microondas microwave
el minibar mini-bar
el minuto minute
el mirador overlook [viewpoint BE] (scenic place)
mirar v look
la misa mass (church service)
mismo same
los mocasines loafers
la mochila backpack
molestar v bother
la moneda coin, currency
mono cute
la montaña n mountain
el monumento conmemorativo memorial (place)

morado purple
el mostrador de información information desk
mostrar v display
la moto acuática jet ski
la motocicleta motorcycle
movilidad mobility
la mujer wife, woman
la multa fine (fee for breaking law)
la muñeca doll; **~** wrist
el músculo muscle
el museo museum
la música music; **~ clásica** classical music; **~ folk** folk music; **~ pop** pop music
el muslo thigh

N

nacional domestic
la nacionalidad nationality
nada nothing
nadar v swim
las nalgas buttocks
naranja orange (color)
la nariz nose
necesitar v need
los negocios business
negro black
nevado snowy
la nevera refrigerator
el nieto grandchild
la niña girl
el niño boy, child
el nivel intermedio intermediate
no no
la noche evening, night

el nombre name; **~ de usuario** username
normal regular
las normas de vestuario dress code
el norte north
la novia girlfriend
el novio boyfriend
el número number; **~ de fax** fax number; **~ de permiso de conducir** driver's license number; **~ de teléfono** phone number; **~ de teléfono de información** information (phone)

O

la obra de teatro n play (theater)
el oculista optician
el oeste west
la oficina office; **~ de correos** post office; **~ de objetos perdidos** lost and found; **~ de turismo** tourist information office
el ojo eye
la olla pot
la ópera opera
el ordenador computer
la oreja ear
la orina urine
el oro gold; **~ amarillo** yellow gold; **~ blanco** white gold
la orquesta orchestra
oscuro dark
el otro camino alternate route
la oxígenoterapia oxygen treatment

P

padecer del corazón heart condition
el padre father
pagar v pay
el pájaro bird
el palacio palace; **~ de las cortes** parliament building
los palillos chinos chopsticks
la panadería bakery
los pantalones pants [trousers BE]; **~ cortos** shorts
el pañal diaper [nappy BE]
el pañuelo de paper tissue
el papel paper; **~ de aluminio** aluminum [kitchen BE] foil; **~ de cocina** paper towel; **~ higiénico** toilet paper
el paquete package
para n stop; **~ llevar** to go [take away BE]; **~ no fumadores** non-smoking
el paracetamol acetaminophen [paracetamol BE]
la parada n stop; **~ de autobús** bus stop
el paraguas umbrella
pararse v stop
el párking parking garage
el parque playpen; **~** park; **~ de atracciones** amusement park
el partido game; **~ de fútbol** soccer [football BE]; **~ de voleibol** volleyball game
el pasajero passenger; **~ con billete** ticketed passenger
el pasaporte passport
el pase de acceso a los remontes lift pass
el pasillo aisle
la pasta de dientes toothpaste
la pastelería pastry shop
el patio de recreo playground
el peatón pedestrian
el pecho chest (body part)
el pediatra pediatrician
la pedicura pedicure
pedir v order
el peinado hairstyle
el peine comb
la película movie
peligroso dangerous
el pelo hair
el peltre pewter
la peluquería de caballeros barber
la peluquería hair salon
los pendientes earrings
el pene penis
la penicilina penicillin
la pensión bed and breakfast
pequeño small
perder v lose (something)

perdido lost
el perfume perfume
el periódico newspaper
la perla pearl
permitir v allow, permit
el perro guía guide dog
la persona con discapacidad visual visually impaired person
la picadura de insecto insect bite
picante spicy
picar v stamp (a ticket)
el pie foot
la piel skin
la pierna leg
la pieza part (for car)
los pijamas pajamas
la pila battery
la píldora Pill (birth control)
la piscina pool; **~ cubierta** indoor pool; **~ exterior** outdoor pool; **~ infantil** kiddie [paddling BE] pool
la pista trail [piste BE]
la pizzería pizzeria
el placer pleasure
la plancha n iron (clothes)
planchar v iron
la planta floor [storey BE]; **~ baja** ground floor
la plata silver; **~ esterlina** sterling silver
el platino platinum
el plato dish (kitchen); **~ principal** main course
la playa beach
la plaza town square
la policía police
la pomada cream (ointment)
ponerse en contacto con v contact
por for; **~** per; **~ día** per day; **~ favor** please; **~ hora** per hour; **~ la noche** overnight; **~ noche** per night; **~ semana** per week
el postre dessert
el precio price
precioso beautiful
el prefijo area code
la pregunta question
presentar v introduce
el preservativo condom
la primera clase first class
primero first
los principales sitios de interés main attraction
principiante beginner, novice (skill level)
la prioridad de paso right of way
la prisa rush
el probador fitting room
probar v taste
el problema problem
el producto good; **~ de limpieza** cleaning product
programar v schedule
prohibir v prohibit

DICTIONARY

el pronóstico forecast
pronunciar v pronounce
el protector solar sunscreen
provisional temporary
próximo next
el público public
el pueblo village
el puente bridge
la puerta (airport) gate; ~ door; ~ **de incendios** fire door
el pulmón lung
la pulsera bracelet
el puro cigar

Q

qué what (question)
quedar bien v fit (clothing)
quedarse v stay
la queja complaint
la quemadura solar sunburn
querer v love (someone)
quién who (question)
el quiosco newsstand

R

la ración portion; ~ **para niños** children's portion
la rampa para silla de ruedas wheelchair ramp
el rap rap (music)
rápido express, fast
la raqueta racket (sports); ~ **de nieve** snowshoe
la reacción alérgica allergic reaction

recargar v recharge
la recepción reception
la receta prescription
recetar v prescribe
rechazar v decline (credit card)
recibir v receive
el recibo receipt
reciclar recycling
recoger v pick up (something)
la recogida de equipajes baggage claim
la recomendación recommendation
recomendar v recommend
el recorrido tour; ~ **en autobús** bus tour; ~ **turístico** sightseeing tour
recto straight
el recuerdo souvenir
el regalo gift
la región region
el registro check-in (hotel); ~ **del coche** vehicle registration
la regla period (menstrual)
el Reino Unido United Kingdom (U.K.)
la relación relationship
rellenar v fill out (form)
el reloj watch; ~ **de pared** wall clock
el remolque trailer
reparar v fix (repair)
el repelente de insectos insect repellent
repetir v repeat
la resaca hangover

la reserva reservation; ~ **natural** nature preserve
reservar v reserve
el/la residente de la UE EU resident
respirar v breathe
el restaurante restaurant
retirar v withdraw; ~ **fondos** withdrawal (bank)
retrasarse v delay
la reunión meeting
revelar v develop (film)
revisar v check (on something)
la revista magazine
el riñón kidney (body part)
el río river
robado stolen
robar v steal
el robo theft
la rodilla knee
rojo red
romántico romantic
romper v break
la ropa clothing; ~ **interior** underwear
rosa pink
roto broken
el rugby rugby
la rueda tire [tyre BE]; ~ **pinchada** flat tire [tyre BE]
las ruinas ruins
la ruta route; ~ **de senderismo** walking route

S

la sábana sheet
el sacacorchos corkscrew

el saco de dormir sleeping bag
la sala room; ~ **de conciertos** concert hall; ~ **de espera** waiting room; ~ **de reuniones** meeting room
la salida check-out (hotel)
la salida n exit; ~ **de urgencia** emergency exit
las salidas departures (airport)
salir v exit, leave
el salón room; ~ **de congresos** convention hall; ~ **de juegos recreativos** arcade; ~ **de manicura** nail salon
¡Salud! Cheers!
la salud health
las sandalias sandals
sangrar v bleed
la sangre blood
el santuario shrine
la sartén frying pan
la sauna sauna
el secador de pelo hair dryer
la secreción discharge (bodily fluid)
la seda silk
sediento thirsty
la seguridad security
el seguro insurance
seguro safe (protected)
el sello n stamp (postage)
el semáforo traffic light

163

DICTIONARY

la semana week
semanal weekly
el seminario seminar
el sendero trail; **~ para bicicletas** bike route
el seno breast
sentarse v sit
separado separated (marriage)
ser v be
serio serious
el servicio restroom [toilet BE]; service (in a restaurant); **~ completo** full-service; **~ de habitaciones** room service; **~ inalámbrico a internet** wireless internet service; **~ de internet** internet service; **~ de lavandería** laundry service; **~ de limpieza de habitaciones** housekeeping service
la servilleta napkin
sí yes
el sida AIDS
la silla chair; **~ para niños** child seat; **~ de ruedas** wheelchair
el símbolo symbol (keyboard)
sin without; **~ alcohol** non-alcoholic; **~ grasa** fat free; **~ receta** over the counter (medication)
la sinagoga synagogue

el sitio de interés attraction (place)
el sobre envelope
el socorrista lifeguard
el sol sun
solamente only
soleado sunny
solo alone
soltero single (marriage)
el sombrero hat
la somnolencia drowsiness
sordo deaf
soso bland
el suavizante conditioner
el subtítulo subtitle
sucio dirty
la sudadera sweatshirt
el suelo floor
el sujetador bra
súper super (fuel)
superior upper
el supermercado grocery store, supermarket
la supervisión supervision
el sur south
el surfista windsurfer

T

la tabla board; **~ de snowboard** snowboard; **~ de surf** surfboard
la talla size; **~ grande** plus size; **~ pequeña** petite size
el taller garage (repair)
el talón de equipaje luggage [baggage BE] ticket

el tampón tampon
la taquilla locker; ~ reservation desk
tarde late (time)
la tarde afternoon
la tarjeta card; **~ de cajero automático** ATM card; **~ de crédito** credit card; **~ de débito** debit card; **~ de embarque** boarding pass; **~ internacional de estudiante** international student card; **~ de memoria** memory card; **~ de negocios** business card; **~ postal** postcard; **~ de seguro** insurance card; **~ de socio** membership card; **~ telefónica** phone card
la tasa fee
el taxi taxi
la taza cup; **~ medidora** measuring cup
el teatro theater; **~ de la ópera** opera house
la tela impermeable groundcloth [groundsheet BE]
el teleférico cable car
el teléfono telephone; **~ móvil** cell [mobile BE] phone; **~ público** pay phone
la telesilla chair lift
el telesquí ski/drag lift

la televisión TV
el templo temple (religious)
temprano early
el tenedor fork
tener v have; **~ dolor** v hurt (have pain); **~ náuseas** v be nauseous
el tenis tennis
la tensión arterial blood pressure
la terminal terminal (airport)
terminar v end
la terracotta terracotta
terrible terrible
el texto n text (message)
el tiempo time; ~ weather
la tienda store; **~ de alimentos naturales** health food store; **~ de antigüedades** antique store; **~ de bebidas alcohólicas** liquor store [off-licence BE]; **~ de campaña** tent; **~ de deportes** sporting goods store; **~ de fotografía** camera store; **~ de juguetes** toy store; **~ de música** music store; **~ de recuerdos** souvenir store; **~ de regalos** gift shop; **~ de ropa** clothing store
las tijeras scissors

DICTIONARY

la tintorería dry cleaner
el tipo de cambio exchange rate
tirar v pull (door sign)
la tirita bandage
la toalla towel
la toallita baby wipe
el tobillo ankle
el torneo de golf golf tournament
la torre tower
la tos n cough
toser v cough
el total total (amount)
trabajar v work
tradicional traditional
traducir v translate
traer v bring
tragar v swallow
el traje suit
tranquilo quiet
el tren train; **~ rápido** express train
triste sad
la trona highchair

el trozo piece
la tumbona deck chair
el turista tourist

U

último last
la universidad university
uno one
la uña nail; **~ del dedo** fingernail; **~ del pie** toenail
urgente urgent
usar v use

V

las vacaciones vacation [holiday BE]
vaciar v empty
la vacuna vaccination
la vagina vagina
la validez valid
valioso valuable
el valle valley
el valor value
el vaquero denim

los vaqueros jeans
el vaso glass (drinking)
el váter químico chemical toilet
vegetariano vegetarian
la vejiga bladder
vender v sell
el veneno poison
venir v come
la ventana window
el ventilador fan (appliance)
ver v see
verde green
el vestido dress (piece of clothing)
el viaje trip
el vidrio glass (material)
viejo old
la viña vineyard
la violación n rape
violar v rape
el visado visa (passport document)

visitar v visit
la vitamina vitamin
la vitrina display case
viudo widowed
vivir v live
vomitar v vomit
el vuelo flight; **~ internacional** international flight; **~ nacional** domestic flight

Z

la zapatería shoe store
las zapatillas slippers; **~ de deporte** sneaker
los zapatos shoes
la zona area; **~ de compras** shopping area; **~ de fumadores** smoking area; **~ para picnic** picnic area
el zoológico zoo
zurcir v mend

INDEX

Airports 114
Ayuntamiento 26

Banco de Valencia 45
Baños del Almirante 35
Barrio del Carmen 36, 88
Basílica de la Virgen de los Desamparados 35
beaches 115
bicycle hire 115
Bioparc 48
bullfighting 92

Cabanyal 65
Calle Caballeros 36
Calle de la Paz 42
Calle Isabel de Villena 64
camping 117
car hire 117
Casa Museo de José Benlliure 50
Catedral 29
    Els Balconets de la Seu 34
    Miguelete 31
    museum 31
    Puerta de Hierros 30
    Puerta de los Apóstoles 32
    Puerta del Palau 30
    Water Court 33
ceramics 71, 83
Ciutat de les Arts i les Ciències 57, 94
Colegio del Patriarca 46
Corpus Christi 91
Cortes Valencianas 36

Dehesa 71
Denia 78

El Corte Inglés 81
El Palmar 71
embassies 121
Estación del Norte 25

Fiestas 88
food and drink 84

Galería del Tossal 38
Gandía 75
Gulliver statue 55

Health 124
hotels 137
huerta 11, 66

Iglesia del Carmen 37
Iglesia de los Santos Juanes 39
Iglesia del Temple 54
Iglesia de Santa Catalina 29
Iglesia de Santo Domingo 54
Instituto Valenciano de Arte Moderno 49

Jardin Botánico 49
Jardines de Monforte 53
Jávea (Xàbia)
    church of San Bartolomé 79

La Albufera 71
La Lonja 41
Las Atarazanas 62
Las Fallas 26, 35, 89
L'Hemisfèric 58
L'Oceanogràfic 59
Los Viveros 53
L'Umbracle 59

Manises 71
Mercado Central 40, 82, 84
Museo de Bellas Artes 52
Museo de Cerámica de Manises 71
Museo de Ciencias Naturales 53
Museo de Historia de Valencia 48, 94
Museo de la Ciudad 35
Museo de la Imprenta y de la Obra Gráfica 73
Museo del Carmen 38
Museo de les Ciències Príncipe Felipe 58
Museo Fallero (Fallas Museum) 56
Museo Nacional de Cerámica González Martí 42
Museo Taurino 26
Museu Prehistòria i de les Cultures de València 50
Museu Valencià d'Historia Natural 49

Palau de la Generalitat 35
Palau de la Música 55, 86
Palau de les Arts 87
Parque de Cabecera (Capçalera) 48
Paseo de Neptuno 63
Paseo Marítimo 63
Peñíscola 74
Plaza Cánovas del Castillo 29
Plaza de la Reina 28
Plaza de la Virgen 34
Plaza del Ayuntamiento 26

INDEX 167

Plaza del Mercado 39
Plaza de Toros 26
Plaza Porta del Mar 54
Plaza Redonda 28, 82
Port 62
Portal de Valldigna 37
post office 27, 130
public holidays 131
Puente de Calatrava 54
Puente del Mar 55
Puente del Reino 56

Raco de l'Olla 70
Real Monasterio de la Trinidad 51
Real Monasterio del Puig de Santa Maria 72
River Turia 10, 56

Sagunt 74
Santa Catalina (Café) 29, 104

Tavernes Blanques 72
Torres de Quart 38
Torres de Serranos 50
transport 134

University 45

Xàtiva (Jàtiva) 77
  castle 77
  municipal museum 78
  San Feliu 77
  San José 77

Berlitz pocket guide

VALENCIA

Fifth Edition 2018

Editor: Carine Tracanelli
Author: Nick Inman and Clara Villanueva
Head of Production: Rebeka Davies
Picture Editor: Tom Smyth
Cartography Update: Carte
Update Production: Apa Digital
Photography Credits: 123RF 4ML, 5MC, 45, 70, 76, 90; Alamy 1; Bigstock 15, 94; Corbis 19, 21, 22, 72; Corrie Wingate/Apa Publications 5T, 5TC, 5M, 6R, 11, 13, 26, 29, 33, 34, 40, 47, 50, 53, 57, 79, 86, 102; Getty Images 4TC, 37; iStock 5M, 5MC, 7, 7R, 17, 24, 31, 38, 43, 44, 55, 59, 61, 63, 67, 68, 75, 83; istock 4MC; Joanbanjo 64; Shutterstock 4TL, 6L; SuperStock 104; Valencia Tourism 49, 69, 80, 84, 89, 93, 97, 99, 101
Cover Picture: iStock

Distribution
UK, Ireland and Europe: Apa Publications (UK) Ltd; sales@insightguides.com
United States and Canada: Ingram Publisher Services; ips@ingramcontent.com
Australia and New Zealand: Woodslane; info@woodslane.com.au
Southeast Asia: Apa Publications (SN) Pte; singaporeoffice@insightguides.com
Worldwide: Apa Publications (UK) Ltd; sales@insightguides.com

Special Sales, Content Licensing and CoPublishing
Insight Guides can be purchased in bulk quantities at discounted prices. We can create special editions, personalised jackets and corporate imprints tailored to your needs. sales@insightguides.com; www.insightguides.biz

All Rights Reserved
© 2018 Apa Digital (CH) AG and Apa Publications (UK) Ltd

Printed in China by CTPS

No part of this book may be reproduced, stored in a retrieval system or transmitted in any form or means electronic, mechanical, photocopying, recording or otherwise, without prior written permission from Apa Publications.

Contact us
Every effort has been made to provide accurate information in this publication, but changes are inevitable. The publisher cannot be responsible for any resulting loss, inconvenience or injury. We would appreciate it if readers would call our attention to any errors or outdated information. We also welcome your suggestions; please contact us at: berlitz@apaguide.co.uk
www.insightguides.com/berlitz

Berlitz Trademark Reg. U.S. Patent Office and other countries. Marca Registrada. Used under licence from the Berlitz Investment Corporation

Berlitz®

speaking your language

phrase book & dictionary
phrase book & CD

Available in: Arabic, Brazilian Portuguese*, Burmese*, Cantonese Chinese, Croatian, Czech*, Danish*, Dutch, English, Filipino, Finnish*, French, German, Greek, Hebrew*, Hindi*, Hungarian*, Indonesian, Italian, Japanese, Korean, Latin American Spanish, Malay, Mandarin Chinese, Mexican Spanish, Norwegian, Polish, Portuguese, Romanian*, Russian, Spanish, Swedish, Thai, Turkish, Vietnamese
*Book only

www.berlitzpublishing.com